MOTHER ON

A catalogue record for this book is available from the National Library of New Zealand.

Soft cover ISBN 978-0-473-62316-6

Soft cover POD ISBN 978-0-473-61875-9

Hard cover ISBN POD 978-0-473-61876-6

Kindle ISBN 978-0-473-61878-0

epub ISBN 978-0-473-61877-3

Design & layout www.yourbooks.co.nz

Printed in New Zealand by www.yourbooks.co.nz

This book has been printed using sustainably managed stock.

MOTHER ON

Honest and healing poetry and prose about mothering on
through the thick of the early days.

With love

EMMA HEAPHY

This book is dedicated to my husband and children, who have helped me find the words by living, loving and crying through this chapter with me.
I love you.
I love you.
I love you.

Contents

Introduction

Dearest Reader,

Welcome to the pages of my heart and mind.

Mother On is the second book in my early motherhood collection, following my debut *Dear Motherhood*. Within these pages, you will find honest and healing poetry and prose about the continued journey through the thick of the early days with young children.

My first book carries the reader from pre-pregnancy through to life with two children. This book is a flow-on from that, including many of the same stages of motherhood, now relived, as well as new stages I have experienced for the first time. It adds new perspectives and helps fill in more of the never-ending gaps that this season brings.

By way of background, I am a mother of two with a third baby on the way. We live in New Zealand, and are privileged to experience a rural lifestyle. I am a Stay-at-Home-Mother who is now also working from home. What started out as scrap notes on my phone during night feedings with my eldest has now become a reasonably busy business. And like motherhood, I am constantly learning along the way.

What I have found through my motherhood journey is that mothering doesn't necessarily get easier, but we learn to adapt better to the hard. And so, I have written this second book largely to give space to those of you who may no longer be new at mothering, but still face many new challenges.

My hope for this book is that the musings remind you that you are supported, you are seen, and you are not alone in your continued motherhood experience. But most importantly, I hope that through my words you find the power you need on any given day to mother on.

With love,

Emma xx

Motherhood

[Mamaaaaa!-hood]
NOUN

Where everything you do is led by love.
Where everything you feel is because of love.
Where everything you need is found through love.
And it can often feel so heavy, so heart-wrenching, so vulnerable.
It can often feel so raw.
Because it is these things.
This is what it is to have your whole world glued together by love.
This is what it is to share the beat of your heart.
This is what it is to love with every breath.
This IS motherhood.

*Definition from: the dictionary of my heart.

CHAPTER ONE

PREGNANCY

*You are not just a vessel. You are a lifeline. And because of you,
someone gets a chance at living. Remember that.*

Two lines

I remember it so well
Waiting the recommended time
Nervous on the toilet seat
Praying for two lines

Will this be it?
Or will we have to start again?
Please be it, I'm ready
I even have a name

I turn the test over
And my heart skips a beat
Is that one line or two?
I shuffle on the seat

I choke on my relief
As I see more than one
Overcome with excitement
I'll be someone's mum

I then stall for a moment
To process this big news
Will they be a boy or a girl?
And when am I due?

Tears start to flow
My cheeks shiny and red
As I realise how lucky I am
For the road lying ahead

I take a deep breath
Then leave, stick in hand
Putting it in a special place
Rechecking it on demand

I then keep myself busy
But mostly in my head
And still the day goes slowly
My impatience being fed

I want it to be 5pm
So I can share this special news
Or perhaps I should just call him?
My mind can't seem to choose

I manage to restrain myself
And the time finally arrives
I greet him with our two lines
Towards him my body dives

We stand huddled together
I feel his excitement in his hold
Speechless about what this means
Leaving dinner to get cold

Eventually it sinks in
And the talking doesn't stop
The anticipation of what's to come
Stays firmly at the top

But we know the depths of this
We discuss what can go wrong
We know nothing's guaranteed
What we've previously undergone

Even so, it's a privilege
To experience this incredible start
To get a chance to have life
Grow directly from your heart

All we can really do
Is take it day by day
Hoping that we get there
And that all will be okay.

Our body

My body is ours
You've made it your home
A perfect fit for your needs
My heart, blood and bone

You'll stay safe here
For nine months of growth
I'll give you my all
So you get the most

It's under construction
With changes every day
New lines, different sizes
Many which will stay

And I don't always love it
But I'm trying my best
Know I love you
That's not part of this test

To me you are perfect
In every single way
And although we haven't met
It's easy for me to say

You fill me with love
And I feel like I'm home
With you growing inside me
My heart's never alone

We're in this together
Through every little part
And what a privilege it is
To be your start

And although you'll leave
My body missing you
It'll remain your home
The place we both grew.

Roller coaster

Pregnant Mama,

This is hard, isn't it? And beautiful.
But mostly a big mix of both.
I don't know how you're feeling, but I'm tired, wired, ravenous, not
hungry, uncomfortable, emotional, over it, into it, and everything in
between. No consistency of any sort exists right now. Some days are
more hard than beautiful, and other days are more beautiful than hard,
but that's okay, because one day soon we'll get to hold such beauty in
our arms and feel the most consistent sort of love we've ever known.
How could that not be worth all the hard?

And how are you holding up? Or not?
I hope you know it's okay to be both.
It takes a lot to grow fingers, toes, little lashings of hair, a heart and a
brain. We're literally growing a heart from our own. That's incredible.
Remarkable. Nothing short of a miracle. It takes a lot from us, then we
give from what we don't have. Breaking, then rebuilding, over and over,
is part of this, okay?

And are you taking photos? Or forgetting?
Some weeks I do both.
I just want to remind you that even though we may not feel beautiful,
or up to it, or like we want to remember some of the moments in this
season, our future selves will thank us for documenting the parts we can
manage. The good, the hard, and the mundane. We will look back on
them one day and see ourselves in a much different light. One of pride
for what we got through. For what our body gave us. For who we were.
And that baby, or toddler, or child that's too big to carry will eventually
want to see where they started. We were their beginning. How could
that not be beautiful?

And are you feeling like you are doing too much? Or somehow like you need to be doing more?

I feel both, constantly.

There doesn't seem to be a middle ground. Perhaps that's because growing a human from scratch is one of the most extreme things our bodies can do. It is the epitome of productive. It's no wonder we are feeling like we're doing too much, by doing nothing else. Remember that, okay?

Pregnant Mama,

It's a roller coaster for you and me both.

But when our day arrives,

What a story we'll get to tell, and a happy ending we'll get to experience.

Behind the scenes

They don't see everything.

They see the two pink lines.
The excitement of the news.
The ultrasound photos.

They see the announcement videos.
The beautiful bump updates.
The gender reveals.

They see the baby shower cupcakes.
The fruit comparisons.
The countdown week by week.

They see the social media updates.
The new baby.
The newborn photo shoot.

But what they don't see are your negative pregnancy tests.
Your previous losses.
Your anxiety as you try again.

What they don't see is your head in the toilet.
Your feet swelling underneath you.
Your hormones ruining you.

What they don't see are the days bedridden.
The nights awake.
The weeks of wishing away the hard.

What they don't see are the tears.
The rage.
The incomprehensible guilt.

What they don't see is the discomfort.
The restlessness.
The worry about what's coming next.

What they don't see is the pushing.
The pain.
The cutting and stitching.

What they don't see is the ongoing bleeding.
The sheer exhaustion.
The overwhelm with all the new.

What they don't see are the hours on demand.
The lack of sleep.
The broken mother.

Behind the scenes there is such sacrifice, such perseverance, such
resilience.
There's a mother pushing through the hard to bring beauty, love, and
life.
There's a mother who doesn't just stop when the bump photos do.

They don't see it all.
But you know it all.
You have lived it all.

Mama,
Don't forget your behind the scenes when everyone else does.
Getting through it is an amazing achievement,
And you should be so proud.

Two chapters at once

Pregnancy is different when you have other children to care for already. It's a miracle, and no less special than your first, but it's where the splitting of your attention starts. Holding them in your arms is simply where it continues.

Every mother knows pregnancy is sacred and that the life inside of her is worthy of celebrating, even if her body is pushed to the limits. And it's hard every time, but it's a different type of hard when you have others already at your feet.

It's having little people asking you to pick them up, to find their toy, to play hide and seek when all you want, and all your body needs, is to rest.

It's getting up at night to feed, rock, or care for those same babies who needed you during the day, with the one inside of you twisting and twirling for your attention.

It's mothering on while growing another you will mother, knowing that you only have a certain window of time to enjoy your now before everything changes.

It's two chapters needing to be read at the same time, even though the characters are introduced at different times.

And it's feeling like there's never enough time to enjoy both seasons fully, no matter how hard you try.

But despite all of that, it's also a different kind of special.

It's having your older children kiss your belly and talk to their yet-to-be-born-sibling through your stretching skin.

It's having such a special time in your life shared with the most special people in your life.

And it's knowing where this sort of love story can take you in a few months.

This sort of pregnancy is a roller coaster of a different kind, physically and emotionally, no matter how many times you have ridden it. But it's the kind that makes you even stronger as you ride it and more content as you finish it. It's the kind that makes you realise you can read two chapters at once, and still end up with the most beautiful ending.

A new love

I'm having a baby,
And it feels like you're still a baby.

You're so small, and dependent.
Your body still fits inside the outline of mine.
Our nights still lead us to each other.

You're so young, and vulnerable.
Our time together has only been short.
Your needs still as many as they once were.

You're so completely naive to what's coming.
But I want to tell you,
Even though you won't understand just yet.

I want to tell you that Mummy is having another baby.
He or she will be smaller than you,
And will live in our house with us,
And will want lots of my time, day and night.

But this new baby is not to replace you, okay?
You are your own.
What we have, and will continue to have, is our own.

But our life will be new.
The new will become part of yours too,
It already has.

You are bound by the closeness of me carrying you both.
You on my hip.
He or she in my tummy.
Every time you hold me, you are holding them too.

And you will see that what awaits us is the best kind of new,
Eventually.

That closeness will become one of playing together, learning side by side,
and holding each other through childhood and beyond.
It will be one of sharing me, but feeling full of love.

That ache you have for me will become an ache you have for them.
It will become a bond you carry for life.

That new little person you may struggle with at times will become all
you feel you know.
They will become something you'll never want to lose.

So my baby,
Mummy is having another baby.

Yes this means change for us,
But it also means a new love for you.
And I can't wait for you to believe me one day.

Trusting that I do

I have moments that come over me right now.
When I'm getting up at night to cuddle my little boy back to sleep, forgetting how many times I've been up already.
When I'm holding my toddler who is having a hard time with her emotions, my own hanging by a thread.
When I'm cooking dinner with the two of them trying to climb up my legs and into my arms, which are already preoccupied with hot pots and pans.

In these moments I worry.
I wonder, "but how?"
I sink into the realisation that this will all be even harder soon.

My mind takes me to unhelpful places.
I struggle to foresee how this will all work with another child in the mix.
I get fixated on the fact that I do not have enough arms already and the mental load is already so heavy.

And I forget.
I forget that other mothers have had more children for centuries.
I forget that I was a new mother of one and a new mother of two myself, and I adjusted eventually.
I forget that, like my eldest did when my youngest was born, my older two will adjust with me, but in their own time.
I forget how much stronger I have become through every stage so far, and how that will help me through the moments of weakness to come.
I forget that my love for my children makes me realise capabilities in myself I never knew existed.
I forget all the times over the years I have said "I can't" when I have, proving that "I can".

I forget,
I already know how.
Not because I have been in this exact stage which awaits me, but because
I have moved through many stages before.

I know I will get to where I need to by lowering my expectations even
more.
By understanding that it will be harder, but I'll have the easiest reason to
face it.
By letting my love for them lead the way through the storms, and their
love for me lead me in the direction I need to keep moving: forwards.

I know it always works out in the end.
That no matter how challenging it gets sometimes, I will say "I wouldn't
change it".
That this is something I may not feel ready for just yet, but my heart will
always be prepared for.

I know it.
I do.
I just need to remind myself in these moments to keep trusting that I do.

My destination

I don't know you yet.
I don't know the colour of your hair, the shape of your nose, the size of your smile.
I don't know the sound of your cry, the smell of your head, the way you like to be settled.
I don't know what your skin feels like, who your features remind me of, how you wish to find your way into my arms.
And I'm so excited to find out.
To meet you. To hold you. To get to know more than what my imagination tells me.
It's felt like a long road sometimes, without many stops to enjoy you, me constantly being needed by your older siblings throughout.
Yet at the same time it feels like only yesterday when I found out that you were the direction I was going.
And what a journey it has been.
You've made it easy to find you when I've been lost in the hard.
I know the route to you like the back of my hand.
And do you know what?
I'd travel it again.
This much I do know.
Because you are the destination.
And I've been to similar destinations before.
They have different names, but the love I have for them is the love I have for you.
So big, nothing can come close.
Little one, I don't know you yet,
But I know where we've been so far,
I know where we are now,
And I cannot wait to see where we are going.

It's time

After nine months, there comes the time when it's nearing "the time".
And no matter how many times you've done it, it feels completely new.

It's the waiting.
It's the excitement.
It's the worry.
It's googling everything.
It's wondering "is this it?" over and over.
It's holding onto your older babies a little tighter.
It's the overthinking.
It's the awe.
It's the having no idea what's coming.
It's the nesting.
It's the endless toilet breaks.
It's the sitting because you can't stand any longer.
It's the insomnia.
It's the birth videos.
It's the sending of "Not yet" text messages.
It's the frustration.
It's the exhaustion.
It's the tears for no reason.
It's the anticipation for what's to come.
It's the mourning of your current.
It's celebrating your past.

This is the period right before giving birth and every woman who has
been through this before knows it.
It's a lot. It's not easy. And none of what awaits you is for the faint-
hearted.
But that's exactly why you will get through it.
You are strong. You are resilient. You are Mother.

CHAPTER TWO

PREGNANCY LOSS

I'm sorry. I'm sorry. I'm so, so sorry.
You are loved. You are loved. You are so, so loved.

Red velvet

This is for the mother thick in loss.
The bad news echoing in her ears, the tears staining her bare thighs which warm the familiar white seat beneath her.
The questions whirling around in her head, like the storm she wasn't prepared for. The self-blame drowning her.
The repeated tests, just to be sure, leaving her worse off than when she started. A new rip tearing through her broken heart with each one.
The love exiting her body in red velvet. Lighter with each day, but a heavy constant reminder of what she won't have in her arms forever.
The needles bruising her skin every few days. Her arm a pin cushion pierced with her reality which is far different to her dreams.
The new reflection looking back at her, now difficult to face. Upside-down smiles all she can muster as she cradles what was meant to be such happiness.
The carrying on, despite her pain. The showing up for her work, or her other children, or life's other demands, because she has to. All the while completely lost in her hurt.
The mother who has been here before, or repeatedly since the start.
The mother who is broken. Hurting. Lost in her very own nightmare. This is for that mother.
And if you are her, or can see parts of her in this,
I hope you know that you are loved.
I hope you know that you are strong.
I hope you know that you are not alone.

Keep swimming

Pregnancy loss challenged me in more ways than I could have imagined.
It was a very difficult time in my life.
There were so many feelings, questions and hormones that I was
unprepared for.
I felt completely out of my depth.
I wanted to sink, not keep swimming.
My body was at odds with my mind.
My heart helpless to my body.
My womb a place of hurt.
No one could have prepared me for that.
So if you have gone through, or are going through loss, I see you.
I see your pain. Your hurt. Your broken heart.
And please, please, keep swimming.
You're worth it.

Have had

We didn't get to meet you
Or hold you like we should
We only have two lines
A story misunderstood

I know it happened quickly
Before you grew too much
But you were there, our baby
A love we couldn't touch

And we were so excited
To add to our family
We pictured you here with us
For all eternity

But life had other plans
Which we couldn't control
And that made it hard
The pain took its toll

People tried to help us
To ease this emptiness
But sometimes all they did
Was add to my distress

They'd say "it happened early"
Or "at least you know you can"
"You've got one already"
Or "you can try again"

I didn't want to hear this
It discredited my ache
I just needed validity of
My pain through heartbreak

Because you were our baby
You were so loved too
But others didn't always get
Just what we've been through

You'll always be with us
A special memory, close by
We'll treasure our time forever
You are part of our why

We love and miss you daily
With the time we didn't have
You were another life, our love
A special baby we have had.

Silent embrace

One thing we should all strive to be comfortable with, is sitting with others while they are hurting, and understanding that sometimes talking isn't the answer.
It's recognising that sometimes the biggest form of comfort you can offer is the willingness to sit in the uncomfortable with them.
It's appreciating that sometimes it's your silence which says the most.

CHAPTER THREE

THE FOURTH TRIMESTER

Like that precious bundle in your arms, you are a newborn too. Take your time to adjust. Enjoy your baby. Love on any other children you may have. And whatever you do, prioritise finding the strength to put boundaries in place to allow yourself to do these things. Your family needs you right now, not endless visitors.

Gateway

Moments after giving birth to our second child, my husband saw me exhausted and overwhelmed with every emotion possible.
And in love. So in love with the baby we created, I grew, and brought safely into the world.
And I remember it.
I felt so tired but powerful.
So raw but relieved.
The aftermath was wrapped in euphoria.
I was immersed in the calm after the storm.
And there was so much love and excitement in that room.
It was bursting into the corridors of nurses and other midwives.
It was cluttering the inboxes of those patiently waiting for the news.
It was exhausted whispers between us, as we all got to know each other through the sweat and tears.
We had done it. I had done it, again.
And while it was the end, it was really only the beginning.
Because birth is the gateway. I was the gateway.
And that exhausted mother is still there.
Now adorned in comfy maternity clothes and robes during all hours of the day and night.
Exchanges often still in whispers, now in darkness.
Sweat and tears falling in moments of too-muchness.
I'm still there.
Months after the gateway opened.
After the fourth trimester ended.
After the excitement dulled down.
I'm still there.
And I'll always still be there because a love like this never fades.
Not like my exhaustion will one day, eventually.
My love only grows.
And I grow with it.

Just us

It was the moment
Of calm post-storm
You on my chest resting
Snuggled into my warm

It'd been a long road
Of changing and growth
Our two bodies as one
Working us both

It felt like a lifetime
Of being your home
Nine months then over
The fourth unknown

I'd waited for this
Of just us in quiet
The moment of meeting
Whispers in private

I felt your soft skin
Breathed in your scent
I kissed your wet forehead
Into your heart I leant

I told you my name
And assured you "I'm here"
Before telling you yours
Gently in your ear

I listened to you
As you conversed with me
Little grunts, tiny breaths
My heart felt free

Nothing else mattered
At this point I knew
You were my whole world
And I was yours too

So we stayed for a while
In this bubble of us
Making most of our time
Before others would fuss

I gazed at you
As you focused on me
It felt like time stopped
So we could just be

But when the end came
And there was a line
To celebrate your entry
And hear about mine

I held on tightly
To these moments of us
So tight I'll never forget
When we were just us.

A new everything

I see you Mama,

Baby in your arms
Dishes in the sink
Waiting for a moment
To get up and have a drink

Washing piles around you
Your phone is close by too
The TV's been on for hours
Yet everything feels new

Still in the padding
Clipped bras on rotate
Moving still hurts a little
Under that soft extra weight

Swallowing your tired
Trying to offer your best
As visitors keep calling in
When all you want is rest

Adding to your lists
Seeing what's to be done
Forgetting that right now
You're someone's number one

Up late in darkness
Down for a short time
Running on empty
With no space to unwind

Wearing your new skin
Covering up the marks
It's easy to forget
That you are pure art

You are always needed
It's easy to feel touched out
You watch time move slowly
Your needs going without

Your mind is always on
Juggling other's needs
Appointments, laundry, love
Hungry mouths you need to feed

It's just so relentless
You rarely get a break
I know your body feels
That tired, full ache

But this won't be forever
This stage shall soon pass
And one day you'll miss
These special firsts and lasts.

Permission

Newborn Mama,

You are allowed:
To say "no" to phone calls
To say "not yet" to visitors
To say "yes" to your needs

You are allowed:
To say "I need help"
To cry about everything
To whinge about nothing

You are allowed:
To feel "touched out"
To not want to hand them over
To ask others to pass them back

You are allowed:
To feel overwhelmed
To feel underwhelmed
To feel both at the same time

You are allowed:
To rest
To ignore the mess
To clean if that's what you want

You are allowed:
To be moody
To feel resentful
To not understand how you are feeling some days

You are allowed:
To have boundaries
To get to know your baby alone
To silence everything that causes you stress

You are allowed.
Because this is your baby.
Because this is an important time in your life and the start of someone else's.
Because you will never get this time back, but there will be more time for everything else.

You are allowed and you should.
Because this is hard.
Because you need to make it easier for yourself.
Because your feelings matter too.

The unsaid

Mama of more than one,

You have been here before, but it's different this time, isn't it?
You have a new baby.
A sore body.
And much healing to do.
Just like you were when you had your first.
But you also have other children to tend to on top of that.
So you have less energy.
More guilt.
And a whole raft of demands from others who need you too.

Your body is even more tired as well, isn't it?
It's older than before.
It's been stretched once again.
It takes more time that you don't have to heal.
Yet despite this, it's not like when you had your first, is it?
Your phone isn't as loud.
Your freezer still has room.
The visitors are less.
And so you are doing more.
You are resting less.
You are carrying on despite your body screaming at you to take your time.

No one talks about this.
This change when you have a new baby but it's not your firstborn.
Perhaps it's because people think that when you've already had a child, you know what you're doing.
Or maybe it's because it's not considered as big of a milestone as the birth of your first child.
Either way, it happens.

So here is what no one says but everyone needs to hear:
A subsequent baby is just as important as the first.
They deserve to be celebrated and supported in just the same way.
And a mother who has given birth again is in just as much of a need, if not more, for love, care, and an extra set of hands.
Please show up for them.
They both need you.
Now, and perhaps more than ever.

Tired privilege

What it is to be here with you.
A tired privilege.
A fatigued beauty.

Your soft skin against mine,
Hearts melting into one.

Your tiny hands grasping to my skin,
Mutual needs echoing in the dark.

Your perfect rise and fall,
Steadying as it finds slowness in my touch.

What it is to be here with you.
Whispers in two.
Together as one.

Working to find sleep,
Time dissolving into our embrace.

Tears wiped away,
Carrying each other through storms.

Finding our way,
Darkness shared between only us.

What it is to be here with you.
My world, your home.
My "rod", your need.

Being everything to each other,
While we can right now.

Doing nothing other than holding one another,
While we fit like a puzzle.

Having our broken sleep shared,
While putting the pieces of each other back together.

What it is to be here with you.
To be this tired.
To be this needed.
To be this broken.

But also,
To want to stay here forever.

The dark side of deprivation

What they don't always tell you about sleep deprivation:

It hurts.
Everything hurts.

Your eyes burn.
Your back aches.
Your arms shake.

You feel trapped inside a cycle of tired,
But you have no choice but to keep going.
Nothing about it is in your control.

Your thoughts can be dark.
They can be intrusive.
They worry you.

Actually you worry about everything.
You overthink.
And there is no perspective to serve you.

You are emotional. So emotional.
Things set you off that normally wouldn't.
The tears fall but can be hard to catch.

Nothing happens quickly enough.
And everything is too loud,
Including your own voice.

You can feel lonely.
Isolated.
And resentful.

You can become a shell of who you normally are.
Almost lifeless,
With your life dictated by the hours at night.

Every minute becomes calculated.
You develop anxiety about the minutes you miss.
And all of a sudden you have insomnia when you get the rare
opportunity to sleep.

You often fuel your body with the wrong foods.
And then feel worse.
But have no capacity to change it.

You can withdraw from your friends.
Your family.
Your life outside of mothering.

You can struggle like you never have before.

Sleep deprivation is no joke.
It can be debilitating.
But because it's wrapped in so much love – the reason for it IS a love
like no other – it can feel hard to talk about.

Sleep is a basic human need.
Without it we do not survive.
And with little amounts of it, it's really hard to function.

Support the mothers you know who may be in the depths of it.
Help them to see the light at the end of the tunnel.
Because it's there, but right now they may not be able to see it.

Season of variables

There is no medal for how you feed your baby.
There should be no place for pedestals.
There should be no talk of which way is best, better, right or wrong.
It is not a competition.
Motherhood is not a competition.
And while it may feel like it sometimes, it never will be.
Because it's not fair to compare when all variables are so different.
Every baby is different.
Every mother is different.
Every family situation is different.
It's about doing what's best with your variables.
That's it.
However you feed your baby is valid.
Whatever reasons you have for feeding your baby the way you do are valid.
And your way, which is the right way for you, your baby and your situation, is no one else's business.
Period.

Entire story

Mama, I'm so grateful for you.

You are my beginning. You brought me to life. You are the reason I'm here. You have done so much for me already.

You look in the mirror and see someone new. New lines, new marks, new skin. But that's all I know. That's all I love. That's everything about you that reminds me of our journey.

You may look different now, but I hope your new reminds you of our journey too.

Mama, I'm so grateful for you.

You are my middle. You carry me each day. You are the reason I smile, grow and love the life I'm learning. You are why I'm learning. You do so much for me every day.

You tell others that you're tired and need a break. But you don't tell me that. You get up for me every time no matter when. You do everything for me all the time when there's no time for just you. You always put me first.

You may feel like you come second right now, but not to me. You are my first too.

Mama, I'm so grateful for you.

You are my end. You are the last person I see before I fall asleep, or reach my place of calm. You are the reason I end my day with a smile and want to start a new day seeing you first.

You say you're worried about our firsts becoming lasts, but please don't worry. The lasts mean new firsts together and the memories of them will last forever, I promise.

You may not want to see the end, but you will always be my beginning.

Mama, right now you are my entire story.

You are my beginning, my middle and my end.

And I'm just so grateful for you.

CHAPTER FOUR

BODY IMAGE

*There will be new pieces of yourself that you will pick apart.
There will also be older pieces you try to fit into. Your body is
always going to be a work in progress. But what it won't always
be is someone else's home.*

Her now

Pre-children, her stomach was the least favourite part of her body.
She thought her belly button was always too big and the scars from her
teen piercing unflattering.
That was closely followed by her legs, due to varicose veins which
worsened as she played more sport into her early twenties.
Then there was her hair. It was always so thin, and never parted where
she wanted it to.

And the pre-children version of her would have been alarmed by this
new version of her, had they met.
A version that came with her becoming a mother.
A version that was not normalised.
A version she was not prepared for.
Her stomach now marked with the lashings of growth, her belly button,
the tightest part of it all.
Her legs now covered in purple rivers that flow from her hips to her
ankles, the banks forever trying to burst in the heat.
Her hair now lost, not thin, parting in no way but with her head.

But thankfully they didn't meet.
And thankfully the her now is not the her then.
The her now has changed in every way possible, and has moved inward
towards what really matters,
Her heart, her mind, what her body gave her.

She's trying to normalise the new parts of her for herself and for her
children,
Because they are the sum, the result, the full price paid for age, for
sacrifice, for this sort of love.
And most of all she realises that by honouring herself now, she's also
honouring them forever.
Because without the new that she now wears, she wouldn't have them or
her new life she's created.

I knew her then,
And I know her now,
Because I am her.
But they only know her now, not then.

So, I choose to honour her now.
I choose to show her.
I choose to love her now and forever.
Because she's given me the most.
She's given me my forevers.

Mirror of beauty

I see the way you look at me now.
It's not the way you used to.

We don't have as much time anymore.
I understand that.
Some days we don't see each other until the final moments before bed, as
we brush our teeth and reflect on all of the tired.

And you hardly look at me, even though I don't want to take my eyes off
you.
It's like you don't want to see me anymore.
But to me you are still beautiful.
A different beauty yes, but worn by the same you I have always loved.

I love the new.
Like the lines around your eyes when you smile. They are because
of what you have given us. The tired you go through for them. The
sacrifice. The happiness. I just wish you would let me see them more.

And the marks on your stomach and legs. The ones you struggle to show
me. They are permanent reminders of how much your body has done
for you, for us. But also, of how much it has stretched beyond limits for
love. And to me they are exquisite art. Life painted on you for keeps.
They deserve to be in a gallery. I hope you can see them the way I can
one day.

And the empty patches on your hair line, with handfuls of leftovers falling into the sink. They may not come back. I know that you worry about that. You tell me, as you brush what you have left into yet another new part. I know it's hard. But I wouldn't notice if you didn't tell me. I'm too busy trying to catch your smile.

And then there's the softness of your edges, which you now cover up in oversized clothing. I don't need you to tell me it bothers you. I see it does as you try on your old clothes sometimes. You toss them in a pile behind you, while you sit in your own heap of upset. Please size up more. Your softness deserves to fit. It is your softness that represents so much more than a number.

There's so much I see when you let me.
So please let me see you more again, like you used to, before we had children.
I want to remind you that these changes are beautiful and worthy of love.
I want to show you how much confidence suits you.
It's just I need you to take the first step.

Love,
Your reflection.

Still

My boobs aren't what they used to be.
I have dimples on the cheeks below my waist.
My posture is terrible.
I have marks of stretch tattooed over my stomach.
Veins weave over my legs.
I'm a few sizes up.
Wrinkles don't only show when I smile now.
The dark eyes seem to be here to stay.
I have grey hairs.
And patches without hair.
I smell of children. But it's not always the good kind of smell.
I have a pouch.
I'm softer to touch.
And I definitely have one strong arm.
I'm not the woman I used to look like, or feel like, or smell like.
I'm the tired, aged, mothered version.
But that must still be beautiful.
How could it not be?
My children grow here too.

The skin I'm in

Body of mine, thank you.
Thank you for being the home to my children.
For being a safe place for them to form, and grow, and leave into the real world.
For trusting that I can do it, and pushing through when my mind has told me I can't.
For stretching, and accommodating, and then stretching some more.
For forgiving me for what I have fed you, unhealthy food and comparison included.
For telling me when I've needed to rest, but allowing me to dig into your reserves when I have no other choice.
For showing me how powerful I can be, how resilient I am, how much I can do.
For being there for me through it all.

Body of mine, I have put you through so much.
Numerous pregnancies.
A loss.
Births.
Back-to-back fourth trimesters.
Yet you have kept showing up for me.
You carry me every day in all of my forms.
You are the core of my current season,
Because without you, I wouldn't have them.

I know I don't say it enough, but thank you.
You are the skin I'm so grateful to be in.
And I vow to keep showing up for you too.

Document now

Mama,
Even if you feel tired,
Self-conscious because of the tired,
Or that your best angles cannot unearth the beauty from all the layers of
tired,
And even if you do not love your changed body,
Your new skin,
Or the clothes that cover an unfamiliar softness you are trying to get to
know,
Get in the photos with them.
Capture yourself in the moment.
Document all of the tired, the new, and the softness.
Because you may not feel perfect, but to them you are, exactly as you
are.
And you deserve the reminder,
One day, if not today,
That all that tired, all that sacrifice, and all that selflessness,
Was actually your kind of perfect too.

CHAPTER FIVE

PAST THE FOURTH

*Just because you may no longer be considered a "new mother",
doesn't mean you no longer need support. You may have more
experience, but you're still learning. Your needs may change,
but they are still valid. You don't deserve to be forgotten.
Postpartum is forever.*

Beyond

I'm still in postpartum clothes, stained and stretched.
I'm still wearing my hair whichever way is easiest, messy and practical.
I'm still healing post birth, undoings forever hidden under the doings.
I'm still up feeding him every few hours day and night, exhausted and worn.
I'm still carrying him everywhere, his littleness heavier and arms stronger.
I'm still changing nappies and soaking spills, repeated and relentless.
I'm still anchored at home mostly, under him and on top of nothing.
I'm still drinking too much coffee and living off love, cup empty and heart full.
I'm still learning so much about us, him first and me second.
I'm still tired.
I'm still hormonal.
I'm still in a bubble of love.

Yet it's not still the newborn phase.
Or the fourth trimester.
It's 6 months postpartum.
And 3 months past the fourth.
But it's also zero months.
It's zero months past the stage of still being needed.
It's zero months past the stage of still being there.
It's zero months past still being his still.

There are still mothers everywhere in the fifth, sixth, seventh and tenth trimesters.
Tired eyes and wakeful babies.
Sore bodies and postpartum lapses.

Doing much the same as in the fourth,
But they don't get any title, or classification or justification other than
"tired Mama".
And they don't get the same support,
Other than from the hands that will always be there.
They can feel washed away in the tides that keep crashing.
Forgotten in memories that they are still making.
Unimportant in the work that remains of the upmost importance.

Mama, who is past the fourth,
I see you.
You still matter.
You may not get the privilege of a number anymore,
But remember you are still someone's number one.

Labour of love

No matter how you feed your baby, it's a labour of love.
By breast,
By bottle,
By both.

It's labour because it's hard work.
And we're all working hard.
We're getting up at all hours to tend.
We're trying to stay awake, nodding heads startling us.
We're all doing what's needed to feed our babies days in, nights out.

Whether that is endless nursing bras in the wash and nipple shields on
the feeding table.
Or the constant sterilising of breast pumps and labelling of freezer bags.
Or the preparing of bottles containing formula or breast milk and the
pre-night-shift organisation of them in the fridge.
Or all of that.
Each way is labour.
Each way is love.

And my way was exclusively breastfeeding.
We'd been going for 7 months.
And sometimes it felt more like labour than love.
Like in the beginning when I felt the sting of every latch, the toe-curling
rawness still fresh in my mind.
Like when I was getting up every hour to feed him at the four-month
regression, the life I gave him in darkness leaving me feeling lifeless all
day.
Like his later need to feed off me in his sleep and not take any bottle
awake, the heaviness of his dependence sometimes weighing me down.

And in these moments, I would sometimes think, "It's time to stop.
I can't take the constant drain on my body.
The depletion.
The touched-out storm that crashes into me".
Then I'd express.
Persist unsuccessfully with the bottle.
And consider weaning cold turkey then and there.

But I didn't.
Because he wasn't ready.
And I wasn't either.
I knew this because I was still pulled back in.
I felt uneasy at the thought of it ending.
I'd put the expressed milk in the freezer for another day.
I'd feed him to sleep and surrender to his needs.

And in the moments of the two of us in the dark, quiet ambience of his
nursery, immersed deep in each other's peace, I was relieved that we were
still going.
It felt like more love than labour.
It was a whole bottle of what I needed to keep going.

So Mama, if you're still feeding your baby, no matter how you're feeding
your baby,
I see the labour and the love.
It's a lot sometimes.
And you can say that.
You're giving a lot.
It's your love giving life.

My "harder"

For me?
The newborn stage is hard, but the baby/toddler stage is harder.
My newborns slept reasonably well.
They fed reasonably well.
They were not overly fussy.
They did not have colic, or other health difficulties.
And as a freshly postpartum mother, my births had been straight forward.
I didn't have any serious birth injuries or trauma.
I didn't suffer from postnatal mental health issues.
I've always had a supportive husband.

And of course, these are not the only factors that make something easier or harder.
There are so many factors.
Too many to count.
But on the whole, the newborn phase for me has been okay.
Doable.
Not as hard as what comes next.
And I'm grateful for my newborn experiences.
So grateful.
As well as for the privilege of my "easier".
But with every "easier", there is a "harder".

As we move through the baby stage, the sleep starts to get shorter and less consistent.
I start to get more tired.
The teething is what always triggers the start of some tricky roads to navigate.
I'm up with them as many times as some others are in their newborn phase.
I'm still sending messages at 3am and sleeping until they wake in the mornings.
I'm forgetting things, apologising for things, needing so many things.

And then comes the big emotions as we enter toddlerhood.
I struggle with them the most. I always have.
I'm constantly fighting the urge to get triggered by their upset, their own
"harder".
And it's tiring.
It adds to the tired.
It is another layer of what-I-struggle-to-find-the-energy-for-today.

And these are times where I question the strength of my mental health.
As I struggle to wade through the exhaustion from a teething baby or
an overtired toddler and keep trying to be the mother I put so much
pressure on myself to be for them.
And at this point, I'm no longer freshly postpartum, or in the fourth
trimester, or a newborn mother.
At this point, the expectation seems to be that the "harder" is over.
That my body should have recovered.
That my babies should be sleeping through.
That I'm more equipped for the big emotions.
And as a mother who is no longer "newly born", things around you go a
little quieter, even though it can be deafening in your own world.
And you become quieter too, because of those very same expectations
you don't want to question.

So, for me?
The baby/toddler stage is more difficult that the newborn stage and for a
long time I've not said this for feeling like I'm in the minority.
For you?
It may be the opposite.
But for every single mother who is reading this, your "easier" and
"harder" are valid.
Don't let comparison or expectations rid you of your truth.
There is no one plot in the story that is motherhood.
And I hope you can find the strength you need to be the author of your
own.

Your answer

You're no longer a newborn
But you still wake up at night
It doesn't make you "good" or "bad"
There is no wrong or right

You're no longer a newborn
But you still prefer me near
Your chest rising on top of mine
Tiny warm breaths in my ear

You're no longer a newborn
But you still cry to communicate
So I'll be here to answer you
Whenever you call, early or late

You're no longer a newborn
But you still search for me
No matter if you're awake or asleep
I'm the light you want to see

You're no longer a newborn
But you're still small as can be
And even when you outgrow my size
Your needs will always fit me

You're no longer a newborn
But you're still so very young
So I'll keep holding you close my baby
Others can bite their tongue

You're no longer a newborn
But I am still your mother
And no matter your stage, I'll be here
Helping your heart recover.

Before I'm ready

The onesies that are now too small remain in his cupboard.
The socks that are now too small remain in his drawers.
The bassinet that is now too small remains in his room.
The play mat that is now too small remains in the living room.
The unused nappies that are now too small remain on his change table.
His now-too-small everything remains exactly where it was.
Because I'm not ready to part with the too small.
I'm not ready to organise the too small.
I'm not ready to make room for the too big.
He's still so small.
It feels like all of the too small now was too big only moments ago.
And he will never be too small or too big for me.
I guess this is my way of holding on.
To the time that has already passed.
And to the time that keeps passing before I'm ready.
But the thing is,
I'm not sure I'll ever be ready.

Everything

I can't leave the room without you crying for me. As soon as I'm out of sight, your heart hurts. It worries that I won't come back. I tell you I'll only be a minute. I need longer sometimes. But I don't take it. I pick you up and we do it together. It takes longer. It's harder. But I choose it because it's easier on my heart.

I can't put you down at night without you needing me later. You search for my skin. I wake immediately to the slightest of whispers. Perhaps it's because we're still as one. I like to think of it that way. I drag myself out of bed on autopilot, search for my robe, and then for your tiny body. I hold you close, as the tired holds onto me. You rest there, and I rest knowing I'm still your safe place.

I can't put you down for more than a few minutes without you begging me to carry you. You don't like feeling like you're missing out. You want to see things from my level. You want to know that I'm still your legs, arms, and priority. It can be hard on me, but it's easy to forget how much you need me right now. So, I remind myself. I carry you. And we carry on being each other's first.

I can't shower each morning without you wanting to get in with me. I shower you with toys on the bathroom floor, but I'm not close enough. You want in too. You try to open the doors, and plead with me to let you in. I turn off the tap, shampoo still not rinsed out and legs half-shaven. You smile as I pick you up with barely a towel covering me, wet footprints on the carpet left in a trail behind us. All you want is me to shower you with my love, time, and care.

I can't do a single thing without you crawling all over me. And I often feel so touched out. So out of touch with myself. Like I'm being suffocated by being needed so intensely. But as we pace the hallway looking at photos of the smaller you, I'm reminded that this intensity won't last. It will fade too quickly. And all we'll have are frames filled with memories of how I wore you for years, and how you were the only outfit that aged, but was timeless.

I can't do much without being your everything right now.
But that's okay,
Because being that is everything to me too.

CHAPTER SIX

TODDLERHOOD

Even if it doesn't feel like it some days, there's still so much love there. And all they really need is for you be the finder and keeper of their heart under all that human.

Leaving it for me

You love me so much.
I am everything to you right now.
You really do love our slow days together.
I know this.
I tell myself this.

But you get bored of waiting for me some days.
You want me to do more with you other days.
You don't like that the more is no longer as much every day right now.
I also know this.
And I don't always like telling myself this.

But I can't always be fun, exciting and fresh.
I can't always do things with just you anymore.
I can't always give you the more you were so accustomed to before.
You don't know this quite yet.
And it's hard to tell the best way to explain.

You express your frustrations on just me.
You save your tears for just me.
And your smiles are stored for those who see you less but can give you the more you so often crave right now.
I'm coming to know this.
And I'm telling myself I'm doing my best.

You do this because you know you can with me.
You do this because I'm your safe space, your sponge that is never too full to wipe up and hold your spills.
You do this because you know I'll never get bored of being there for you however you show up.
I know it.
And it's a tell-tale sign we're on the right track.

So, while you leave me with the spills, the tears and the less-than-easy more than others.
And while it can be hard not to question myself when this happens.
There is no one better than me to receive those parts of you because I know you better than anyone.
And I know that's all that matters.
No one can tell me otherwise.

Answering you

"Just ignore it", some say,
As you cry and grizzle for me,
"Mum, mum, mum", you plead between tears.

"Just leave her", some say,
As you scream in a heap on the floor,
Your arms trying to find their way to me.

"Just you wait 'til she's three", some say,
As I refuse to ignore it, or leave you,
Answering your needs wherever they fall.

Why?
Because I can't just ignore it.
I can't just leave you.
I can't just wait 'til you're three.
I'm with you every day.
I'm living with it every day.
You are my every day.
And no matter the day (or night),
I feel it with you.

Hearing you cry is painful,
Your pain is also mine.
Hearing you scream is distressing,
Your distress is also mine.
Hearing you call for me is pulling,
Your calls are mine to answer.

So I answer to you,
Not them.
And I'll probably be judged by some,
Not you.
And when you're three it may be harder,
Not sure.

I'm not sure about much really.
Perhaps that's because we're always moving through uncharted territory together.
Your firsts are also mine.

But I am sure that how we approach our firsts will be different to how others approach theirs,
And there should be no catch-all right or wrong.
It's about doing what feels right for us.

And my little lady,
Because you are still so little,
It feels right to go to you,
To answer your needs,
To be there.

And my darling girl,
Because you are still a darling,
What works for you right now feels right for me,
And what works for me right now feels right for you.

And my eldest baby,
Because you are still my baby,
I don't think I need to wait 'til you're three to figure that out.
Even if I could, that just wouldn't feel right for us.

Carrying love

I still carry her sometimes.
Some say too much.
But I carry on and carry her.
Her feet nearly at my knees, her age two and a half, nearly three.
Even though she can walk, and run, and carry things on her own.

I still carry her, making things harder for me and easier for her.
I still carry her, with her perched on one hip, incorrectly formed
sentences echoing in my ear.
I still carry her, and more than just her weight when she's in my arms.
I still carry her.
When she wants to be carried.
When she needs to be carried.
When she reaches out to me with her now-longer arms and says, "Mum,
up, up, up" with her now-shorter patience.

I lift her up.
I bring her close to me.
I carry her like she's still my baby.
Because she is still my baby.
She will always be my baby.
A baby who one day will carry herself by choice.
A baby with height, and "cool" clothes and a cell phone that she doesn't
call me on as much as I'd like.
A baby who, when she wants to be carried, may choose to be carried in
the arms of someone other than her mum.

So, I still carry her.
Around our kitchen, the shops, and at the end of every walk.
Because regardless of age or size, or whether we can get from A to B on
our own, we all need and want to be carried sometimes, don't we?
Because regardless of the load we are carrying ourselves, we all like the
load to be shared or carried for us sometimes, don't we?
Because regardless of what others think, allowing ourselves to still be
carried sometimes is important, isn't it?

I still carry her because I want to teach her this.
I want to normalise sharing the load, and allowing herself to be carried
sometimes.
I want her to value herself enough to know that being carried sometimes
is never a weakness.
Because as women we carry a lot.
Some say too much.

So, I carry her now.
I will carry her when she lets me.
And I will always carry more than her weight whether she needs me to
or not.
In my mind, my heart, my every breath,
I will carry her forever.

The touch

My toddler fell asleep on me while I was carrying her.
Her legs dangled past my hips, and her arms flopped over my shoulders.
She is getting heavier these days, and my back breaks when I carry her
for too long, but I didn't want to put her down.
Because this almost never happens anymore.
All the nights of us dancing, with her little body on mine in darkness, is
now only a memory.
What used to be a tiresome need for me at all hours, is now bittersweet.
So I didn't put her down.
I held her close.
I held onto the moment as tight as I could.
Because these moments are so special now.
They take me back.
They hold me in what won't always be.
They remind me that, for now, I still have the touch.

Big girl

"I'm a big girl now"
She tells me as she puts on her (s)"cool bag" and her boots that look
just like mine.

"I'm a big girl now"
She tells me as she holds the chalk herself and draws squiggly lines
which are apparently "us" (the people, the pets and Peppa Pig in our
little family).

I'm a big girl now"
She protests as she pushes her trolley around the house, filling up her
imagination, and emptying out the pantry.

"I'm a big girl now"
She says proudly, as she brushes through her now-shorter hair, because
big girls get haircuts, "Okay Mummy?!"

"I'm a big girl now"
She tells me when she wants to get her own breakfast.
When she wants to brush her own teeth.
When she wants to get herself changed.

"I'm a big girl now"
This is what I hear when she wants to do something on her own.
When she thinks she can do everything on her own.
When she doesn't want me to help her with anything, even the things
she cannot yet do on her own.

"I'm a big girl now", she says.
And I hear it,
Although I'm not close to being ready enough.

But I'll keep hearing it.
I'll hear it when she wants me to.
I'll hear it when she needs me to.
Just like I heard it today, before her first day at kindergarten.

And I'll keep telling her "you are a big girl" with a smile on my face and a lump in my throat.
Because this is what she wants to hear.
But I'll also keep telling her that while she's bigger, she's still my little girl.
I'll keep telling her that she can do as bigger of things as she wants to.
I'll keep telling her that no matter how big we all get, we can all still feel like that same little girl we once were.
Because we can.
We should.
That's what it is to be human.

And as my "big girl" went to her first day at kindergarten, I felt like the little girl she was leaving behind.
"I'm a big girl now, Mummy", she said with a smile as we drove to the drop off.
"You are, my darling", I told her.
"Mummy is having to be a big girl today too."

Big little emotions

Toddler Mama,

It can all seem so hard some days.
A type of hard that you are never really prepared for.
So quickly you can feel so out of your depth.
So defeated.
So helpless.

As the emotions rise, the tears fall.
Sometimes of you both.
And that's okay.
You are allowed to find it all too much too.
Those emotions are so big.
Even though they are so small.

And while it's hard not being able to fix their hurt, or be their answer,
It's even harder feeling like you are to blame.
But you are not to blame.
This is not about you.
Their hard is not your doing.

You are doing enough.
You are more than enough.
You are the perfect amount of enough.

That's why they save it for you.
When the day hasn't even begun.
When you feel like you're the one needing saving.

And that's why they come back to you.
When the dust has settled and the tears have dried.
When everything else isn't too much for them anymore.

Because you are never too much for them.
Or too little.
You are just right.

And they know that you will be there for them.
Through the hard.
Through the too-muchness.
Through all of it.

So, it may not feel easy.
Far from it.
But you make the hard easier for them.
Go easy on yourself, okay?

The you yet to come

First you were one
That start year for us
The birth, postpartum
Taking time to adjust

There were long hours
Up all night and day
Which turned into teething
Then your first taste of purée

I saw your first smile
You roll onto your tum
Then sitting on your own
Your first "Mama" and "Mum"

I remember you crawling
And giggling with joy
The sound of your cry
Your favourite soft toy

Then you turned two
That second year of us
The tears, the emotions
The making a fuss

You were walking by then
And asking me things
You dropped a day nap
Started spreading your wings

Then you gained pace
And an interest in shows
You'd put words together
Like your choice in clothes

You'd feed yourself
And brush your own teeth
But when you wanted help
My lap was your seat

Now you are three
And that third year of us
Has been and gone
Without time enough

You'd stay up too late
And want to "come too"
You'd hate missing out
On the old or the new

You liked to play more
And tell others your name
You'd share your toys better
And join in on the games

Yet you'd still enjoy cuddles
Making sure I was close
I still loved that too
Probably the most

So here we are now
This fourth year of us
I'm not sure what's coming
There's no plan, as such

But you'll keep growing
Learning as you go
Time will move quickly
And I'll want it to slow

You'll lead the way
With me alongside
Witnessing your next year
Which you'll take in your stride

My darling I'm proud
Of who you've become
And I can't wait to see
The you yet to come.

Patience is a virtue

You wait for them to become, to be here, to grow before your eyes and in your arms.
To learn, to flourish, to share in their youth.
To smile, to laugh, to sit then crawl.
To speak, to sleep through, to walk then run.
To share, to play fair, to relax on their own.
To need less of some things, to do more of others, to stand on their own two feet.
Then all of a sudden, the waiting is over without warning.
All of a sudden, it's too late to see the last.
All of a sudden, you would do anything to wait for them to grow bigger a little longer.
Mama, when there is a wait, there is still time.
Enjoy having to be patient.

CHAPTER SEVEN

MOTHERING MORE THAN ONE

Having more children means more mess, more late nights, more early mornings, more chaos, more tired, more sacrifice, more hard days, but it also means more love. That's why we do it. Love always wins. Love always makes it worth it.

From one to two

When you go through the transition from one to two, you can
experience waves of guilt about your newly split attention.
You want to spend more time with your eldest who is adjusting to their
new normal.
And you also want to soak up every single moment with your newborn.
But it's simply not always possible to do both.
And that can be difficult.
You can often feel washed away by the guilt.
But there's something bigger at play.
Something that often cannot be seen until a while later,
A few weeks or even months on.
Something worth waiting for.
And that something is them to each other.
They grow into it, just as you do.
They fill the gaps where you can't.
They give each other a completely new type of love.
A type of love which overflows and is capable of drowning out the guilt,
if you let it.
So let it.
Because you did that.
You gave them each other.
And for that, there's absolutely nothing to feel guilty about.

Our mould

There's only one of me
And I can feel not enough
My posture ruined, arms too short
As I try to share my love

One needs a drink of milk
The other wants a kiss
And then there's still the rest of it
On my never-ending list

I ask one to "wait please"
So I can tend to the other
But they have no understanding of time
Or what it takes to be a mother

So I do what I can
With the hands I do not have
Their tears belting, my stress heightening
All of me they try to grab

My heart is torn in two
Upset by having to choose
Between the loves of my life
One should not have to lose

The waves crash down on me
With a guilt I've come to know
And it's multiplied by the chorus
Of "Mama" being echoed

But this is mothering
When you have more than one
This is being shared completely
Before the day's even begun

And when these moments pass
As they do eventually
I'm pleasantly reminded
Being torn was temporary

Cos when I'm not spread thin
And they both have me to hold
I realise my all is all they need
I AM enough for our mould.

Still here

I'm still here, okay?

I know it's different these days.
We are not alone as much anymore.
You miss me.
I can tell that.

And let me tell you,
I miss you too.
I miss you both,
Even when we are together.
Especially when we are together.
Because I know I can't give you both what you need all the time,
And you both crave me.

But your craving is particularly deep right now.
It's a need for all of me.
All of my time.
All of my attention.
All of what we used to have.
Before you became the eldest, and I became stretched.
Before two became three.

And that's okay.
You can miss me.
And I can miss you.
It doesn't mean we don't love being three,
Or that we would change now for anything.
It just shows how much we love each other.
How special our time was as two.
That we are lucky to miss each other at all.

But I know this isn't always easy for you.
I know you have days where you struggle more than others.
I do too.
Because even though you love being the eldest,
And you get upset when you don't know where the youngest is,
You just want to know that I'm still here.
That I haven't forgotten you.
That we are still the same.

I see the change when we can find moments as two again.
I can hold you with all of me,
And you can embrace me with all of you.
These moments are special.
I feel it too.

I am still here.
I promise.
I always will be.
And what we have is still the same, just different.

Thank you for missing me.
And please know, I miss you too.

There you were

You were my first.
The one who came here and showed me the way.
The one who carried me as much as I carried you.
The one who made me a mother.

And everything was so new. So big. So utterly beautiful I wondered if it
was real.
But it was real.
So real I felt the most fragile I ever had.
Like I could break into a million pieces at the thought of everything I'd
never worried about before.

And sometimes I did break.
The sheer love was so overwhelming at times; the tiredness a beast I'd
never known.
But there you were.
In all of your littleness.
Piecing me back together, with your adoration, your perfection, your
unknowing ability to heal with a glance.

You have always been there.
Through every stage.
The hard. The heavy. The heartbreakingly beautiful.
Both yours and mine.
And I'm just so grateful.
For you. For this. For what we have stepped through together.

You were my first baby.
And you always will be.
Even after I've taken my last breath.

Second firsts

My second child,

There's so much I want to tell you.

I remember you in my arms for the first time. Like it was my first time all over again. Like it was yesterday. But it's today and you are months older. I'd normally wish for more time with you, but you have taught me to live for now.

I hear you over the big little noise that drowns you out at times. I see you through all of the distractions. I feel your heartbeat through mine, now torn. You have helped me to learn that I can do even more with the same number of hands, ears and eyes. You are the more, never less.

I hold onto the moments of just us, and live them for as long as I can, because they are fleeting but the memories of you will not be. They are etched into my soul. You are etched into my soul. Next to her, not behind her, or in second place. You have shown me that there are no placings here.

I love you with everything I have, and with everything I don't have some days. It takes a lot from me, but you give me more. Because while the love is shared, it is there in full amounts. You make my heart full. You have shown me that I can love so much that I overflow.

And I know that you did not make me a mother.
And that your firsts are often my seconds.
But you have done something incredible.
Something that comes with being the child second by birth only.

You have helped me to find more of the mother I wanted to and lose
some of the mother I needed to.
You have helped me to see my seconds differently.
And you have given me some of my important firsts.

Only you could have done that.
Only us, together in this way and in this timing, could have made this
possible.
No one else.

And I just want you to know that.

Love Mum x

Unprepared, but right

I wasn't prepared for how much the transition from one to two children would shake me.

I wasn't prepared for missing my eldest, when she's with me, or my youngest when I'm not with him.

I wasn't prepared for how much time I would never be able to find.

How late I'd be up at night or how early the day would start.

I wasn't prepared for how much I'd be stretched mentally and physically. How two hands are not enough sometimes, or how there's never enough room in my mind.

I wasn't prepared for how much I can't get done on top of being their everything. And how much that would test me some days.

I wasn't prepared for how much easier it feels with just one of them for a while. How that actually feels like a break, which isn't.

I wasn't prepared for how much more I'd need from my husband.

How much of my "less than" he'd need to embrace and his trying I'd need to celebrate.

I wasn't prepared for how touched out I'd feel. How taking myself on coffee dates with my thoughts for as much as an hour would help me feel like myself again.

I wasn't prepared for how hard going days on end without a break could be. How much a village proves to be crucial. How much I'd appreciate my friends who I hardly see anymore.

I wasn't prepared for it.

But I also wasn't prepared for how much love I have for them both.
For my family. For being a mother of more than one.
I wasn't prepared for how being a mother of two would shake me loose
and piece me back together in a way I'm so proud of.
I wasn't prepared for how much love they would have for each other.
How much their bond fuels me.
I wasn't prepared for just how much I ache when I think of this being
any different.

I wasn't prepared for any of it.
But I didn't need to be.
Because this is where I'm meant to be.
It feels unprepared, but right.
And that's all that really matters.

CHAPTER EIGHT

FOR THE HARD DAYS

When a mother talks about the hard – a hard moment, a hard day, this hard season – most of the time she is not wanting advice. Almost all of the time she is just wanting to feel seen. And there's a big difference.

Some days

Some days you are so tired your eyes sting, but you get up for them anyway.

You are so overwhelmed you could explode, but you carry on anyway.

You are so fragile you could break, but you keep holding it together anyway.

You are so touched out you could run, but you keep walking beside them anyway.

Some days you just don't feel like it, but you give it your best shot anyway.

And some day they will understand just how much it took to be you.

Some day they will see just how strong their mother really was.

A hard day

After a really hard day, these are some of the things I wrote down:
"Today was so hard.
I felt like nothing went right.
I didn't get anything finished.
No one listened.
I got frustrated easily.
I didn't know how to handle anything.
I felt completely out of my depth.
I should have handled things better.
I felt guilty about how I handled some things.
I got caught up in my own head too much.
I doubted myself constantly.
I didn't enjoy them as much as I should've.
I couldn't wait for bedtime.
I was just so tired.
And so grumpy.
And so irritable.
I wasn't a good mum today."

I wrote these things down because they were the first things I felt and the narratives I fed myself.
But following a night of some sleep, I reflected.
I missed a lot off that list.

This is what I forgot:
"Today's cracks were filled with so much love, attempts, and all I had.
I made them smile and laugh.
I got them through the day safely.
My toddler told me she loved me more times than I can count and my baby wanted to be close to me the entire day.

I love them so much.
I showed up for them, despite being up with my baby most of the night
prior, and up with either or both of them most nights over the last two
years.
I stayed there with them and kept giving them the best I could in every
given moment.
And I continued to be there for them in the hours of light and darkness
that followed.
I was tired because I was tired.
I was grumpy because I felt grumpy.
I was irritable because of being tired and feeling grumpy.
I'm allowed to be these things some days.
These things don't make me a bad mum.
They make me a human who is a good mum."

It's easy to only see the cracks on the hard days.
They seem to stick more.
They seem to hold on for longer.
But don't forget to see the goodness that fills them.
It's always there.
And it's what makes you stronger for tomorrow,
If you allow yourself to see it, write it down, and add it to your list.

Dusting off the hard

Yesterday was one of the hardest days I have had as a parent in a long time.
I felt defeated by 10am.
The tears just kept coming.
Then tantrums.
Then more tears.

I felt like I could do nothing right.
I doubted every decision I made.
I blamed myself for what I felt I did wrong.
And then I kept starting over.
It was draining at best.
And debilitating at worst.

By 5pm I was well and truly spent.
I remember how lifeless I felt.
The last little bit of energy seeping from my pores into them, the
bedtime routine on the horizon.
I had hardly eaten all day, yet I had absolutely no appetite by this point.
I didn't even care for the mess, their untouched dinners or the basket
full of yet-to-be-hung-washing.
I just wanted the fastest route to the closure of the day.

And this is all in the context of being on holiday.
A holiday with my husband and his family supports.
Time away for a much-needed break.
But the children and their dad became unwell.
And despite all supports offered by wider family, my children just
wanted us.
Mum and dad.
But because I wasn't unwell, I stepped up and wore it all, all day.

That's the thing about being a parent.
No matter where you are, you are always needed.
No matter what supports you have, you are wanted first.
No matter what your intentions are for a day, a break, or a holiday, there are no guarantees.
It is the most relentless job on the planet.
And it is not always easy, no matter how easy some make it look.

We all have these days.
We all feel defeated sometimes.
We all know the deep dark moments that these days consist of.
So, here's me admitting defeat, on holiday, with the loves of my life.
Because they are the loves of my life.
Without question.
That's why I get back up, dust off the hard, and keep mothering.
That's why every day I wake up and choose to try and conquer it for them.

But the important word here is "trying".
Because that's all you can really do.
That's all it takes when you are one of the main characters in someone's story.
You just have to try.

Their right

No matter how many things you felt went wrong today.
No matter how many spills, explosions, broken promises, or times you had to clean up the same thing.
No matter how long things took to start or how short the time you had to finish anything was.
No matter how much of only the wrong you chose to see as the last toy was finally packed away.
They won't see it that way.
To them the moments of the messy, the imperfect, the too slow are magic.
They see fun, they see time, they see love.
They see those moments as filled with only what is right.
Because they shared some, most, if not all of those moments with you.
And to them, you are everything.
You are all that is right.

The stage we're in

We go out for coffee and I order it as a takeaway. We get there late, and we almost always have to leave early.

We go to the swimming pools. I have to get into my togs and be prepared to swim with them until they've decided they don't want "in" anymore, rather than sit on the side and watch like the mothers who are past this stage do. Then I get them changed like it's a race against the clock because they are tired, cold, and have suddenly decided they want back in.

We go to the grocery shop. I am rushing to get through as many aisles as I can before a meltdown. I let them snack on the yet-to-be-purchased-item to get us through 'til the end (if I'm lucky), then load the groceries for purchase with one hand, while holding one of them and repeatedly telling them both: "Please don't touch that".

We go out for dinner, rarely. It's just not that enjoyable. The dinner I've been looking forward to all day goes cold while I'm feeding/amusing/ trying to calm an overstimulated child or children. I don't have a moment to catch up with anyone properly, and when we leave I'm almost always covered in something.

We go to the park. They love it. But it's not a walk in the park. I'm pushing them on the swing, then making sure one doesn't fall off the playground, while going down the slide with the other. I'm exhausted by the time we get into the car, but I then have to console tears the whole way home because I decided it was "time to go".

This is the stage I'm in.
We're in.
We still go places.
But right now it's hard.
They need me for everything.
And I get so tired from doing what others may not consider a "big deal".
But these things can feel like a big deal.
Sometimes it's just easier to stay home.

And I know that this will eventually pass.
That I'll be the mother watching more than doing.
That I'll be the mother doing a little more relaxing than rushing.
But I'm not there yet.
And although some days I want to be,
I don't want to be needed less either.

This is the stage I'm in.
It's relentless and all-consuming,
But so very special.
And if you are here too, I get it.
We won't be here forever,
But neither will they.

Temporary

This is temporary.

The tired,
The unfinished coffees,
The everything you have only just restarted.

The loud,
The hormones,
The constant-ness of constant mess.

The hard,
The raw,
The longing for your own time, your hands, your personal space.

It's today
It's right now.
It's temporary.

But the love?
The deepest, truest, fullest love that comes with the temporary,
That's forever.

Let this be the day

Let this be the day you believe that you are doing your best.
The day you tell yourself you are exactly who they need.
The day you remember that imperfect is the goal, and perfect is
impossible.

Let this be the day you realise just how much you are doing by doing
nothing other than being there for them.
The day you celebrate the mess, the unfinished business, the burnt
dinner.
The day you see your worth.

Let this be the day you hold them tight.
The day you hold yourself even tighter.
The day you let go of what you regret and forgive yourself for your
shortcomings.

Let this be the day you tell yourself what you are so quick to tell others,
That you are "doing a great job".

Let this be the day.
And every other day after that.
Until there are no more days left.
Early motherhood is too short not to.

Powerhouse

Mama,
You may not feel powerful right now.
Not physically, as the tiredness drowns you.
Not mentally, as the load weighs you down.
But you are powerful.
The way you calm their worries.
The way you kiss their sores better.
The way you make them laugh.
The way you know what they need, when they need it, why they need it.
And when you don't know, the way you try anyway.
That's power, your power, the power of love.
That is one of the strongest powers there is.
You are a powerhouse.

My person

Mama,

You may not see it, but I do.

I see your effort. You dance around me every minute of every day. You stop what you have just started to get me to the end of what I think I need. And you don't stop until long after my eyes are closed, for however long, each night.

I see your love. You love me so much. I feel it every time you hold me, help me, handle my needs with such care. But I feel it in your struggle too. In your tired, your overwhelm, your little time for yourself, because despite it all, you keep showing up for me.

I see your hard days. They are part of this love story, just as the beautiful days are. And so you wear them on your heart. Next to me. As a constant reminder of how strong you are for getting through them for me. I know you do it for me. I can't wait to tell you how easy you made it to love you.

I see your spark. You light up every room you meet me in. And my smile. My entire day. You are the reason for my happiness right now. Why I wake you up in the night for a cuddle. Why I start your day early to be with you. You are my why. And there is nothing dull about that.

I see your beauty. I try my best to show you. By wanting to be close to you. By holding onto every inch of your bare skin. By letting go only when I have to. I look at you all day because you are my person. My lifeline. My love which is deeper than skin. And that's what makes you so beautiful.

I see it, Mama.
All of it.
And I hope this helps you to see it too.

CHAPTER NINE

FOR THE LONG NIGHTS

*When the sun comes out, your day may have already started.
And when the moon comes out, your day may not necessarily be
over. But this is what it is to be someone's entire world. And this
is what it takes to give them a galaxy.*

Pit of anxiety

Going to bed not knowing how much sleep you may or may not get every night is hard.
It can leave you in a pit of anxiety which tells you how difficult tomorrow will be before it's even started.
It can see you struggling to get to sleep before the night shift has even begun.
But what if I told you that every time you have to rise and tend in darkness, you are one time closer to never having to do so again?
What if I told you that every hold, rock, shush with weak arms is something that is making you even stronger?
What if I told you that every second you spend with your sweet children in darkness is time that you will never get back?
Because this is what that pit of anxiety doesn't tell you,
And you deserve to know.

Warrior

Intentional sleep deprivation has been used as a form of torture for centuries.
Because it works.
People crumble.
People break.
And even though mothers are put through sleep deprivation that is wholly unintentional and a by-product of the choice they make for the life and love they create, it can still feel torturous.
So if you are in the thick of it, keep it in perspective.
It's okay if it feels hard and unbearable some days.
It's okay if you feel like you are about to crumble and break.
Remember, you are not immortal.
But you are a warrior.

The cards we've been dealt

Sleep.
Or rather, lack thereof.

This remains a large part of our parenting narrative.
And I know this isn't uncommon.
That it's normal for babies and young children to not have ideal sleeping patterns.
I also know that this too shall pass.
But it feels like a lifetime right now.
Every night I wonder if tonight will be the night.
Will I wake, but they don't?

It's become such a delicate thing.
When they do sleep, it's precious. A rarity. Something to saviour.
There's so much groundwork involved. So much care, love, and trying to remain calm.
And I'm fragile.
I know what it takes to have to start over.
If my husband comes to bed late, and so much as says a word, I'm at him.
If visitors turn up, I politely but hastily preface any discussion with "just letting you know, that the baby is sleeping".
If I hear the puppy bark, I feel my skin crawling with anxious rage.

I never thought this would be it. Our reality.
And it's not their fault. They are perfect.
It's not mine either, although I sometimes think it.
Our worth is not defined by our children's ability or otherwise to sleep through.
It's just the cards we've been dealt.

But this is what happens when sleep isn't guaranteed.
When there is a challenge to get them down at all, and for them to stay there without needing you again for a reasonable length of time.
It consumes you.
You get better at coping, sure, but it doesn't mean it gets easier.
Because we all need sleep.
We all need breaks to recover.
We all benefit from relaxing a little.
And when you have gone years without any form of solid sleep, it takes its toll.
No matter how much your bones ache with love for them, it just does.

And I say this for a few reasons.
Firstly, to provide comfort to those of you who may be struggling with this right now.
Secondly, to release the anxiety that comes with some of these feelings.
And finally, to one day remember how hard this stage was, but how proud I am for getting through it.

Our time will come.
We will sleep again.
But for now, we'll hold on to what we know will get us through it:
Each other.

Layers of love

Mama,

I know you're tired.
I know you're sick of being tired.
I know you're sick of saying you're tired.
But that's just the way it is right now.

And you know this.
If your baby's tired, you're tired.
Because if they're not getting sleep, neither are you.
Because they are completely dependent on you.
Because you are their lifeline.

And what a privilege it is to be that for someone.
And how amazing it is that someone literally needs every part of you to keep going.
And you wouldn't trade the sleepless nights to not be this for them.
Not ever.
Because they are everything in the world to you.
They are a privilege in all forms.
They are your privilege.

But it's tiring.
And if it's night after night, it can be nauseating.
And the days after days that follow the nights after nights can leave you feeling like you're going to faint in moments of need,
Which is often,
Because you are so needed.
Never in your life have you been so needed.

But it's more than just the tired.
It's everything that comes with the tired.
Because tiredness breeds a lot of unhelpful traits.
Like forgetfulness, irritability, frustration, sadness and overwhelm.
Everything small seems so big.
And nothing big ever feels small

And that's hard.
On them and on anyone else sharing the load with you, where they can, if they can, if your child will let them.
But it's the hardest on you.
It really is.
Because right now, you are wearing layers on layers of tired.
Because right now, you are giving absolutely everything to those who need it from you.
Because right now, you muddle your way through to the end of the day and then carry on into the night.
Over and over.
Again and again.

And I just want to remind you that it's not just you.
I can hardly keep my eyes open right now.
I'm absolutely exhausted from being exhausted.
And it's so hard some days, most days, all day when you feel like this.

But thankfully there are layers on layers of love too.
The layers that cover the tired and uncover our resilience.
They're the layers that keep us going.
Keep going.

nights of us

These are the nights of us
Broken sleep a guarantee
Unsure how many times we'll wake
A game of wait and see

These are the nights of us
Together with the dark
In each other's arms and breath
Tangled from the start

These are the nights of us
Tired with sleep undone
Cuddling close where I find you
Our bodies melt into one

These are the nights of us
A team working together
It doesn't always feel that way
But being there's the measure

These are the nights of us
Tears and dreams are caught
You need me there, but I need you too
You're the tiniest big support

These are the nights of us
Special moments in the tough
The ones I'll always remember
As the diamonds in the rough

These are the nights of us
Love and needs in sync
Undoubtedly the best reason
To hardly catch a wink

These are the nights of us
On call for you whenever
These are the nights of love
A now but not forever.

Someone's comfort

I remember so clearly the feeling of my head falling onto the pillow after a hard day at work, before I became a mother.
There was such comfort in knowing that rest would come.
That all the work of the day would be exhaled as I inhaled the sleep I so desperately needed.

It's not like that anymore.
These days I'm working even harder.
The rest is even more needed.
Yet the time of my head on the pillow is less,
And the comfort of knowing I can catch up on my deficiencies is missing with my sleep.
Because there's work that still needs to be done when my body needs to rest.
It's never-ending work, with forever-ending rest.
It's hard work.

So tonight I'm telling myself,
I'm reminding myself,
I'm comforting myself in the knowledge,
That one day, when I get to reacquaint myself with the comfort of my pillow,
I'll remember how much comfort I was to someone else,
And I'll miss it.

CHAPTER TEN

RESPECTFUL PARENTING

They know the way to our heart, because that was their first home. And they will never forget their way home, if they know they're always welcome there, no matter what.

As they are

Children will be children.
Their behaviour is not an inconvenience.
It's an inevitable part of being young.
So please don't apologise for it.
Their learning, their growth, and their emotional development is
important.
And, like the rest of us,
They have every right to be accepted in society as they are.

Digging deep

Gentle parenting isn't the easier option.
It's one of the hardest things I've ever done.
Because while mothering in the direction my heart points may feel
natural, and intuitive, and "easier" on my heart,
Responding the way my heart wants me to, isn't always what my mind,
my energy, or my time supports me to do.
It's a constant struggle to dig deep within myself to find the gentle, when
the conditions on the surface are layered thick with tired, hormonal, and
touched out.
It's a constant willingness to keep listening to my heart,
When everything else in the moment seems easier.

Only yours to give

My children,
When someone asks or tells you to give them a hug, you don't have to.
You can hug whoever you want, when you want, if you want.
Or you can just not hug at all.
You don't owe anyone, including me, your love and affection.
Right now I'll tell them for you.
And later when you can tell them but don't want to, I'll keep telling them for you.
Because your body, your affection, your love is yours and only yours to give,
Now and always.

For them to know

What I will tell my children.

People won't always agree with you.
Be open to hearing why, and to changing your stance if you feel that's
right, but never mould your opinion to suit someone else's simply
because you don't want to hurt their feelings.
Ripples don't need to ruin the current.
They can be the current for needed change.

You won't always know the right thing to do.
Your gut sometimes isn't loud enough.
And you will make mistakes. Plenty of mistakes.
There will be more mistakes than successes actually.
But mistakes are not failures.
They are growth in disguise.
Welcome them.

You will fall in love one day. Maybe more than once.
You will be heartbroken. Maybe more than once.
You may also break hearts. More than you want to.
And it will be hard, and beautiful in equal measure.
You will feel your heart melt, and then be ripped from your chest.
You will feel the rips of those you hurt.
But love is worth pursuing, keep trusting the melt. It will come.
And when it does, let yourself melt.
Because at the end of the day, love is all we are left with.

Be kind. No matter what.
Be the bigger person. Always.
Remember that other's mistreatment of you is almost never about you.
You don't know what others are going through.
And you don't need to.
All you need to know is that the way you treat others will your biggest asset.
It's worth investing in.

Know your worth.
You are what you put in.
To your work, your family, your life.
But putting in also means putting into yourself.
You must rest. Often.
Rest is productive.
Please remember that.

And finally, not everyone will like you.
They don't have to.
You are not for sale.
And there will be times you do not like yourself.
That's normal.
You are only human.
But I will always love you.
That will never change.

I love you.
I love you.
I love you.

Superpower

I want nothing more in this world than for my children to know just
how much I love them.
So I tell them, without limits.
I hold them, without hesitation.
I show them, without conditions.
Because being loved unconditionally is the most powerful thing I can
give them,
And they deserve to be powerful.

Raising boys

It's okay

My boy,

It's okay.
It's okay to feel,
To hurt,
To ask for help,
To be helped.

And it's okay.
It's okay to hold hands,
To hug,
To be held,
To say "no".

And it's okay.
It's okay to dance,
To sing,
To write,
To explore your creativity.

And it's okay.
It's okay to be wrong,
To make mistakes,
To say "sorry",
To ask for forgiveness.

And it's okay.
It's okay to wear your heart on your sleeve,
To fall hard,
To love even harder,
To be heartbroken.

And it's okay.
It's okay not to drink,
To not enjoy sport,
To not be a "lad",
To not do what everyone else is doing.

And it's okay.
It's okay to be gentle,
To be sensitive,
To be "the kind one",
To still call your mum.

It's okay, okay?
What's not okay is thinking you have to be a certain way, just because
you were born a boy.

Mummy's boy

They say you're a "mummy's boy".
You look for me everywhere.
You cry when I turn my back to you.
You beg me to hold you.

You have a softness about you right now.
And it's beautiful.
So natural.
A reflection of who you are becoming.

You love to cuddle.
You ask for kisses.
You can be so gentle.
And I hope it never fades.
Even when you're older.
Even when you're no longer a little boy.
Especially when you feel like being called a "mummy's boy" is no
longer a compliment.

Because you will always be my boy.
I will always be your mum.
And we will always have parts of each other.

So my darling boy,
My little lad,
My one-day-your-own-man,
It makes no difference.
My arms will always be open.
My heart will always be waiting.
You will always have a key to my front door.

Because I'm your mum.
And no matter what,
I will always love you.

CHAPTER ELEVEN

THE HUMAN IN THE MOTHER

Behind every recipient of "you're nailing it" is a mother who has faced hard days, doubted herself, and cried herself to sleep more times than she may care to admit. No one nails motherhood every day. Some just make it look that way.

The mum they get

They don't get the perfect mum.

They get the mum who can't find the second sock.
The mum who wears her hair up and lopsided always.
The mum who leaves the washed clothes in the washing machine for too long, and the cake in the oven for not long enough.

They get the mum who accidentally dresses them in back-to-front tops and inside-out pants.
The mum who forgets to pack the spare clothes, the sunblock and the pram in the boot before outings that definitely require those things.
The mum who swears sometimes, swears to do better, and then forgets and swears some more too soon after.

They get the mum who is late to most things no matter how early she starts preparing to leave.
The mum who can have stains on her clothes in public and a baby bag which leaves everyone waiting while she spends ten minutes trying to find anything in it.
The mum who sometimes feeds them too much sugar, and not enough greens.

They get the mum who likes her sleep and can get a short fuse when she's tired.
The mum who doesn't always get it right.
They get that mum.

But they also get the mum who loves them more than life itself.
The mum who tries her best with all she has.
The mum who would do anything to give them what they need.

They get the mum who is always worrying for them and overthinking about them.
The mum who shows up, stays there, and never wants to leave.
The mum who sees them completely, even when she doesn't see herself.

They get the mum who thinks nothing in the world can ever compete with what she is privileged to experience right now and the mum who kicks herself every day that they are her reality.
They get that mum too.

There's a lot they get, with me being their mum.
And it may not all be perfect, far from it.
But it's real, it's sincere, it's rooted in complete and unconditional love.
It's me for them, always and forever.
And that's the main thing.
Because there's no such thing as perfect anyway.

The great unlearning

What we are taught to aim for as young women:
Perfection
Order
Punctuality
Selfishness
Efficiency
Productivity
Everything we want

What motherhood asks of mothers:
To embrace imperfection
To let go of ideals
To be patient
To be selfless
To multi-task
To be in a constant state of "pending"
To do everything for everyone else

Motherhood is a great unlearning disguised as a learning.
It's no wonder we question everything some days.
Don't be so hard on yourself.

The measure of love

A mother tries her best to be present in the moment with her children.
So often that is her top priority.
Like somehow her love is measured that way.

And it can be a struggle when she needs to be ten steps ahead.
When she's organising, preparing, thinking about what they may or may
not need when they may or may not need it.
When she's focusing on how she can make the yet-to-be-had moments
be as-best-as-they-can-be moments.

But she's mistaken.
A mother's love cannot be measured solely by her presence in the
moment.
It's not that simple.

A mother's love must always be measured by the moments she makes
happen.
Because those moments are born largely from her presence ahead.
They are born from her constant struggle to juggle her presence to
prioritise her children.

Act of love

Motherhood is buttering toast with one hand.
It's hard.
Everything is served a little torn apart and a lot imperfect.
But we always get it done, somehow.
And that's all that really matters.
Because it's the trying that is the act of love,
Not the perfect.
Because it's the made-with-love that they remember.

Grace

Being tired affects everything.
Your mood, your energy, your overall physical and mental health.
And when you're a parent, this is one of the biggest hurdles you face every single day.
It's wanting to give your children the best version of yourself on the little you have left.
It's the constant intentional act of trying to prevent or limit your tired from dictating your parenting.
It's not knowing when you will get some reprieve from always having to push through.
And some days it's not just hard, its plain impossible.
But on these days, this is not a failing.
This is your body's way of telling you that you have limits.
And quite simply, this is the basis of humankind begging you to give yourself some grace.

- Give yourself grace

Human first

I feel like I'm constantly in a state of chaos.

There are dishes in the sink, laundry is bursting out of the basket, and I find toys in places I've forgotten existed. I'm cleaning when I can, but it remerges. I can't get on top of anything. And it's like this most days.

The windows need a clean, there are cobwebs when I don't look too hard, I need to mop the floors, and the drawers could do with a good sort. And the pantry, the fridge, the freezer, the wardrobes, the filing cabinet. Pretty much everything that stores anything.

And then there's my mind. Constantly on, tabs open, half-closed, reopening, freezing, needing rebooting and starting over. I'm forgetting things. Small things and big things. And I'm feeling guilty about that. I'm trying to write lists, but seeing things not ticked off can be stressful.

I'm wearing the chaos too. I often go without, just like those cabinets, drawers and wardrobes. My self-care is hard to find some days. I try hard, but when the needs of others are so constant, so loud, so lacking in understanding of what it is to be patient, I wait. And when I'm supported to take time, or when I make time, I'm still not ever dedicating that time solely to myself. Those tabs are still open, and I'm still thinking about the chaos that awaits me.

And the thing is, it's hard to sort, or tidy with little children at your feet, wanting to be carried, interrupting you at all times. It's hard knowing that any work will soon be undone. It can be easier to not start. So, I often don't, but the jobs keep waiting, and my mind keeps bursting at the seams.

Until one day I can't handle it.
I can't breathe through it.
And I turn into the grumpy mum.
Then the guilty mum.
Then the sad mum.
Then the "it's just a stage" mum.
Then the mum who keeps going anyway.

It can be hard living in chaos, no matter how utterly beautiful the reason
for it is.
And I think it's normal to feel this way sometimes.
To feel so out of control of everything around you that you lose control
of your calm.
To have to try again better next time.

Surely.
Because you may be a mum,
But you were a human first.

Super Mother, not Superwoman

She's got a million things to do, on her mind, and in her sight.
But she can't do it all.
It's just not possible.
Not today, not tomorrow, and maybe not even cumulatively over the
course of the next few days, weeks, months and years.

But particularly not today,
When she is so needed by the littles who have the biggest piece of her
heart.
When she has little energy to do anything other than love them big.
When the fading time with them is of the essence.

So she reminds herself:
Enjoying them comes first.
Doing everything else comes second, third, fourth, tenth, or maybe one
day.

She reminds herself:
There's no such thing as a superwoman.
One thing at a time, one step at a time, one foot in front of the other.

What we all deserve to hear

Let me tell you what you may not be telling yourself.

You are a good mum. Imperfect moments don't make a bad mother. Perfect in motherhood doesn't exist.

Your children love you as you are, however that looks. Whether that means wearing makeup or not, having fancy clothes or wearing the same thing as three years ago. Irrespective of your size, your hair style, the marks on your skin, they love you.

You are working so hard right now. Caring for your children, playing with your children, and being with your children is productive. Everything that comes with being a mother on top of mothering your children counts too. The mental load is huge. You are carrying so much. I hope you see how strong you are.

Your children will always need you. Maybe not in the way they do now—as their lifeline, their hands, their feet, their voice—but you will remain an important piece of their puzzle. They will not outgrow the need to be loved and supported.

You are allowed to miss your former life some days. Days of yourself, doing things in your own time, and not rushing. Missing them has absolutely nothing to do with loving and being grateful for your current stage. One day, the same will be said for your current.

You don't need to justify your parenting decisions. You don't owe others an explanation for your why. Not now, not ever. But you do owe it to yourself and your children to believe that.

On your hard days, you are seen.
In your long nights, you are seen.
In all of what you do, your love is seen.

So tell it to yourself,
And tell it to every mother you know.
Just tell it.

Because this narrative needs to be told more.
This is what we all deserve to hear.

CHAPTER TWELVE

LOST IN MOTHERHOOD

Despite what society says, you're allowed to be lost in motherhood. To wonder who you are outside of your mothering. To worry about having to find yourself again when this season has passed. Wanting to be in this deep isn't shameful. It's something you can be so proud of.

I am Mother

Who am I now?
I struggle to remember some days.

The photos that flash up as Facebook memories seem so long ago.
I can't remember them like yesterday.

My old sports equipment is collecting dust in the cupboard.
I can't remember the last time I properly used it.

The reflection I never see enough of is so much different than before.
I can't remember who she was.

And I don't realise it much.
I'm too busy being lost in them.

But when I do, it worries me sometimes.
So I take a walk down memory lane, in search of the earlier version
of me.

And I find her.
She's still there.
A younger, more energetic version.

And I still know her, but I don't have much in common with her
anymore.
I'm knee-deep in nappies, I spend nights in, and hardly get the chance to
get out of my pyjamas, let alone put makeup on.
I have very little to talk about other than my children, how tired I am, or
what I'm not doing this weekend.

I'm different now.
A better different.
And I am on a much different journey.

This is life.
This is motherhood.
This is matrescence.

And while I miss the old me sometimes, and that's perfectly okay, the
new me is where I need to be.
I'm the most content I've been my entire life.

I'm a mother.
That's who I am.
And I may be lost in motherhood,
But I sure am finding some of the best days of my life too.

The pursuit of everything

As a mother you can have ideas, passions and things you would like to pursue on top of being their everything.

And you can have everything, or something close to.

I truly believe that.

But only with support.

Because you need time, sleep and energy.

Because without support, a lot of that isn't possible.

And even if it is, it can be at the cost of something else.

Like time with your children,

Or your partner,

Or everything and everyone else needing your time and attention.

So to the mother without supports, or with supports outside of your reach,

And with passions of your own that you can't find the time or energy for just yet,

Go easy on yourself.

You're not failing or falling short.

It's impossible to make everything possible right now.

And it's okay to feel sad, frustrated or whatever you need to about that.

You are allowed to want everything,

Even when you have your everythings already.

What leads us home

I want to have more sleep.
But I don't want to be needed less.

I want to have more time to pursue my own dreams.
But I don't want to miss out on theirs.

I want to have more quality time with my husband.
But I don't want to get behind for tomorrow.

I want to go out all night with friends.
But I don't want to leave my babies.

I want to finish what I start.
But I don't want to begin the end of this chapter.

I want to know they'll always be alright.
But I don't want to overthink everything.

I want to buy something nice for myself.
But I don't want to feel guilty about it.

I want to show them the way.
But I don't want to lose myself in the process.

I want to go on holiday with them.
But I don't want to feel tired the entire time.

I want to have more time in the day.
But I don't want to spend the whole day cleaning.

I want to hang our family photos.
But I don't want daily reminders of how fast it's really going.

I want to do my hair nicely for a change.
But I don't want to be stressed while doing it.

I want to read up on current affairs.
But I don't want to worry myself sick about their future.

I want to do more of what I used to enjoy.
But I don't want to sacrifice the time I won't get back.

I want to relax more.
But I don't want to care less.

I want a break.
But I don't want to miss them.

I want everything.
But I want nothing other than their hearts inside of mine.

I want. I want. I want.
But. But. But.

Overthink. Overthink. Overthink.
Guilt. Guilt. Guilt.

This isn't simple.
Motherhood is not simple.

But wanting to love them is.
No buts, no overthinking, no guilt.

It's the answer to every question.
It's the path that always leads us home.

Where the heart is

It doesn't matter where we are, home is with them.
I am their home, and they are mine.

Where I go, they go.
I drag the tired around with me and they follow, smiles shining bright.
I pull myself through the hard days and they come with me, tears kissed away.
I fall into every day with less than yesterday and they join, seeing only today.

And where they go, I go.
They move into each moment however they feel and I follow, giving them what I can.
They spring into every day and I follow, keeping them safe.
They seek out the love we create and I follow, mirroring and more.

I lead, they follow.
They lead, I follow.
We lead into each other,
And follow each other home.
Every day.
Every night.
Every moment.

Wherever that is.
Whatever that looks like.
Whoever that involves.
It doesn't matter.
Nothing else seems to matter right now.

And there's nothing better than being at home.
Not this sort of home.
Because even when I'm a lump on the floor, giving them life with
the energy I don't have, they give me life too.
And even when they are in a puddle of too-muchness, my less is all
the more they need.
We are the key to each other.

Our home is a pretty special place right now.
Mess, tears, chaos included.
And there's nowhere I'd rather be.

Part of me

Right now they are a huge part of my identity.
I'm lost in them, in every part of them.
They course through my pulse.
They are my pulse, my reason.

And so often I talk of wanting space, to do things without all the extras
that are currently required, to have the weight of only myself to carry.
But I'm all talk most of the time,
Because I feel so empty when they are not with me.
I feel like I'm missing a limb.
I'm completely out of sorts.
I'm not entirely myself when I'm by myself.

That's what happens when you spend every waking hour with your
people.
And they are my people.
My little people.
And their need for me is so strong.
But it's such a mutual need right now.
The strongest one I've ever known.
And by far the most beautiful one.

But it's not going to last, is it?
I won't always be their first.
Sometimes I catch myself thinking about this.
And there's a wave of sadness that washes over me.
And worry.
For them and for me.
I will always worry for them.

But what happens to me?
I'll be a fish out of water, at least initially but probably for a long time.
I'll need to find myself again.
A version which still has them coursing through my pulse, but without
them within inches of my skin.
A small handbag will replace the suddenly empty space on my hip, and
groceries will again fill the empty back seat of my car.

I'm not ready for that yet.
And I don't need to be just yet,
I know that.
But I don't think I'll ever be.
Maybe a little, but not fully.

No one prepares you for this.
To have to lose them a little and find yourself completely again.
To have to find your own pulse after years of breathing in their love.
No one.

And perhaps that's because they weren't prepared either.
Perhaps this is just something no one can ever truly prepare you for.

now

What will I do?
I have no clue
I'm wrapped in you tightly
You are my glue

One day you'll leave
The path that we've paved
The house will be quiet
The beds will stay made

I'll stand in your rooms
Reliving our years
I'll hold your teddies
And swallow my tears

I know I'll be lost
More so than now
My heart needing more
Than time did allow

You are part of me
The extension I know
So when you're missing
I'll need to regrow

It will take time
To sew those seeds
Me getting used to
Re-meeting my needs

I will feel limbless
As I carry on
My load much lighter
But my emptiness strong

It won't be easy
To let you go
But it's what you need
That much I know

This time will come
I'll approach it then
Until then, I'll live "now"
Not in "but when".

Where it started

Mama,
You are literally forming a childhood right now.
You are making memories that they will carry for a lifetime.
You are keeping memories that they may not remember.
And when they get older, all of your often invisible work will become seen.
As you share their childhood memories over family dinners with them, their partners and your grandchildren,
As you immerse yourself in the joy everyone gets from reliving the memories you played a large part in creating,
It will become clear to all.
It started with you.

CHAPTER THIRTEEN

THE OVERWHELMING STRUGGLE

Being a mother is a lot. The load is heavy. The needs are relentless. But you are not limitless. You have a capacity. You can't do it all. Stop. Breathe. Recognise the scrabble in your mind. That's your sign that you are at capacity. Not your sign that you are failing.

Open tabs

Did I send that email? Where's the cellotape? What shall we have for dinner? Did I book the appointment? What's the time? We are running late. "Kids, we are running late." Who has my other shoe? We need more fruit. The washing is still on the line. No time. Mental note for later. Where are the keys? My mask? Did I remind him about the fridge? Did I RSVP to the party? I need to transfer money. Spare clothes. Nappies. Where's the pacifier? Wow I look tired. I should have washed my hair. I need a new bra. Don't forget to take out the rubbish. Was I too distracted last night? Maybe it was taken the wrong way. We need more washing powder. The accommodation is booked, I think? How many do we need to buy for? Maybe they won't like that gift? What dates is he off work? I need to get more books from the library for the kids. And a portacot. And organise the pets. I don't feel so well. I need to eat something. There's no time. I'll take something for the drive. I feel so overwhelmed. What day is it?

- My mind

A different kind of rest

Never underestimate the importance of a mother utilising any time she has, without her children needing her, to do as much as she can before that window closes again.

Rest is important, yes.

And it should be encouraged, yes.

But sometimes a mother just needs to feel in control of her life, or her rarely free hands, or one single thing that won't be interrupted, for her own sanity.

Sometimes that's the only way she can feel rested.

Driver

Here's to the mothers who have cried in the front seat recently.

The mothers who have dropped their children off at day care and left them there distressed for the first time, or so many subsequent times that they've lost count. The ones who held it together as best they could as they assured their child "it's going to be okay", but choked on their own tears as they walked away hearing the cries for them.

The mothers whose upset following drop-off was in complete relief. The ones whose floodgates opened with the realisation that they get a break to breathe again, or work again, or do anything that they haven't been able to do since before the school holidays.

The mothers who have been given some bad news. The ones overwhelmed by how unfair the world can be sometimes. The ones daunted by how they will carry on parenting when they feel broken in pieces.

The mothers who have finally got their children to sleep in the back seat, after driving around in circles for too long. The ones who've then got washed away by every feeling they haven't had a chance to feel since the last car drive.

The mothers who have had a disagreement with their partner, or raised their voice at their children, or just needed to put themselves in their own time-out before they spilled out everywhere. The ones who then spilled out everywhere anyway, rivers of guilt, shame and self-inflicted pressure flowing down their cheeks and dropping onto their lap beneath the steering wheel.

The mothers who have dropped their babies-who-are-suddenly-big-kids off at school for the first time, unsure what they will do with this new time. Or those who have dropped their babies-who-are-suddenly-adult-children off at the airport, unsure when the next time they get to see them will be.

The mothers who needed a release, for whatever reason, for however long it was needed.

Here's to those mothers.

And here's to continuing to let the tears flow,
Even if it's in the front seat.

Because being the driver for this love story is heavy,
And breakdowns happen sometimes.

But is she?

When a mother says "I'm fine", she may be completely fine.
But she also may be sort of fine. Fine today, but she was definitely not fine yesterday.

Or she may be close to fine.
Surviving, but she doesn't want to burden others with the not so fine.

She may be not fine.
Struggling, but she doesn't have the capacity to deal with discussing what's not fine.

Or she may be far from fine.
Drowning, but she doesn't want to admit it to others because then the depths are real.

She may be absolutely anything but fine,
Despairing, but she doesn't want others to worry, or think that she's failing.

"I'm fine."
It has lots of definitions,
But most of them are invisible.

Be kind.
You don't know what sort of "I'm fine" she is.

A cluster of thoughts

Do you ever just think...

I love my kids so much, but I need a break so badly, I'll try to organise one today, but not for too long because I'll miss them, and I'm so tired, I've never been this tired, I wish my children would sleep through, and self-settle, but then I don't want to miss out on being all they need, time is going so fast, wow, was that photo really taken that long ago? Boy, this morning is going slow, and I have so much to do, things I feel I should do, but I want to play with my kids, and be present, and not care about the mess, but the mess is everywhere, and I do care about how out of control it makes me feel, how am I feeling actually? And my kids? I hope I'm doing a good job, but am I? I love them so much and they deserve the best, but I have no energy right now, and I feel so guilty about that, and the screen time, and the unhealthy snacks, and the fact I've been on my phone around them too much, oh the guilt, but I need this, an escape for a second, I think everyone does it, but I also want to work on something for me, I have so many personal goals, but I want to keep my children my main focus, because they have my heart, it's just that it feels impossible to have it all, and there's not enough time to do it all, or is it just me? I still haven't done the washing, or cleared the bench, and the dishwasher is yelling at me, but so are the kids, and it's so triggering, don't yell, don't yell, breathe, why is this so hard sometimes? But nothing has been more beautiful, and I need to eat something, and do some exercise, and reply to so many already opened messages, and it makes me feel like I'm falling short, that I need to do better, and I'm trying, but being needed by my kids takes time, and I'm so lucky for my time to be spent with them, there is no time like now, but how much time have I just wasted overthinking rather than doing, and being, and loving?

Because same.

On

Mothering is being "on" all the time.

It's making sure they have what they need, before they need it.
It's being there for them, even when they don't know they need it.
It's fixing things. It's teaching things. It's cooking things. It's organising things.
It's being all things all day and all night.

And when you get the opportunity to switch off, you can't.
Not fully anyway.
Because you are still on call.
You are still subconsciously waiting to be needed.
You are suddenly remembering all of the things you still need to do for them that you haven't had a chance to do yet.

Mothering doesn't come with an off switch.
That's where the depth of the tired comes from.
But thankfully,
That's where the depth of the love comes from too.

Unseen

Being a mum is doing all the things no one really sees. The bits behind the scenes, the groundwork, the tiring work.

It's being the fun mum when no one's watching. The dancing in the kitchen with pots and pans mum. The singing to the wiggles and wearing funny things on her head mum. The mum who is laughing when she feels like crying.

It's being the present mum. The reading books to them in a pool of mess mum. The sitting with them, lying with them, and being led around the house by them mum.

It's being the prepared mum. The mum who packs the snacks, the bottles, the nappies, the snugglies and every single thing that may or may not be needed for any outing, big or small. Or the mum who may not have had time to be prepared, and prepares accordingly.

It's being the loving mum. The mum who tends to the tears, the boo-boos, the constant needs of others. The mum who drops everything that may be stressing her, and offers a smile, a kiss and an embrace. The mum who would do anything to make them feel okay.

It's being the mum that most do not see, doing a lot of what goes unseen.

So everyone else often sees the tired, end-result mum.

They see the mum tearing her hair out after 5pm. Who hands them over at the earliest opportunity and asks them to deal with the tears this time.

They see the mum who is short, snappy, and anything but fun.

They see the mum who apologises for being late, explains what went wrong before she got there, and struggles to offer much depth to any discussion.

They see the mum who looks frazzled and messy. The mum who puts them in the high chair so she can sit and drink her coffee while scrolling on her phone for a moment, or ten.

They see that mum more than the other mum mostly,
Naturally and unintentionally,
Because that's just how the meetings fall, and the daily schedules play out.

But Mama,
Even though everyone else may not always see the hidden, invisible work of love, I see you.
I really see you.
I see your groundwork.
I see your whole picture.
Because I'm often there in the shadows of the unseen too.
I'm right there with you.

All that is right

Mama,
Stop what you're doing.
Make everything else wait.
Take a deep breath – remember those?
Find your child.
Hold onto them.
Look deep into their eyes.
Stay there.
Get lost in them completely.
See the beauty.
Feel the love.
Immerse yourself in their connection.
And you will find all that is right.
They hold what's right.
It's there.
It's always right there.
It's just that sometimes you need to remember to look.

CHAPTER FOURTEEN

STAY-AT-HOME-MOTHER

*You are working too. Just inside the home. Without breaks.
Or pay. Or employment support. But with a raft of never-
ending demands. You deserve a promotion.*

What I have done

"I haven't done much today."
But by breakfast,
I've been up throughout the night.
I've made bottles in the dark.
I've fed comfort despite my tired.
I've changed nappies under the moon.
I've sung lullabies.
I've danced around rooms.
I've rocked them back to dreams.

"I haven't done much today."
But by noon,
I've fed snacks.
I've cleaned up snacks.
I've sterilised bottles.
I've fed bottles.
I've changed nappies.
I've brushed teeth.
I've dressed them.
I've re-dressed them.
I've hung out washing.
I've broken up fights.
I've picked up things.
I've picked up more things.
I've fed them again.
I've rocked them again.
I've helped one sleep.
I've attempted "quiet time" with the other.

"I haven't done much today."
But by 5pm,
I've taken them for a walk.
I've explained every single thing they've seen move.
I've carried them back while pushing an empty pram.
I've tried unpacking all of their things.
I've tried feeding them snacks.
I've consoled tears.
I've put my baby down for another nap.
I've tried again after another unsuccessful attempt.
I've achieved none of the jobs I said I would in the nap that wasn't.
I've answered a million questions about what I'm doing.
I've made dinner.
I've fed them my dinner.
I've worn fussiness, and food.
I've carried them in my arms more than I haven't.

"I haven't done much today."
But by 10pm,
I've cleaned up the toys.
I've folded washing.
I've hung out more washing.
I've paid bills.
I've helped my husband with his work.
I've made lunches.
I've written lists for tomorrow.
I've done an online grocery shop.
I've organised a birthday cake.

"I haven't done much today".
But I've done so much today,
I've done everything for everyone.
So much so, I've largely forgotten about myself.

Slow days with them

It can be easy to think that you are missing out right now.
That others are out there doing all the things that you could or should
be doing with your children.
That your mothering is somehow not as fun or full as others and that
you could be doing more.
And it can be equally as easy to think you are the only one missing out
on the things you are not sure you are missing out on.

But I'm here to tell those of you feeling this way that you are not alone.
I'm at home with my children most of the time during the week.
Changing nappies, wearing oversized clothing, washing, cleaning,
preparing so many snacks.
We leave the house for the odd thing, but we are never really out for long.
I work in the gaps and the dark hours of some nights.
And weekends are no different.
My husband is just home more, we get into our pyjamas earlier, and
watch Netflix later.

This is our life right now.
At home mostly, with them.
And I'm unsure if we are missing out, or missing opportunities, but I'm
sure we are not missing out on them.
And if this is your life or something close to it, then solidarity.
Here's to missing out for them, or with them, together.

Option hard

Being a Stay-at-Home-Mum is hard.
People often think it's the easier option.
But there's no easier option when it comes to mothering.

I have a toddler and a baby, less than two years apart. They're home with me every day, save for a few hours a week when my daughter goes to kindergarten. We don't have family where we live. I have a business I run whenever I can to keep feeling like I haven't lost myself completely. My husband has a job which requires a lot from him. I ask a lot of him too.

And this is largely our choice. I get that. I also get that we are in a position of privilege to have this choice at all. But we can talk about all consequences of choices and privileges, including the hard parts.

It can be a lot sometimes. The children and I do every single thing together. And it's incredibly special. But it often leaves me feeling easily irritable, overstimulated, and like I need a break. But the breaks don't come much. My baby doesn't sleep through the night yet. There's not enough time between when they go to bed and when I do, to do something substantive for myself. And when I do, it feels like it's always cut short, or not enough.

Some days, like today, I have been cried at since 6am. I've called my husband to vent. And then I've told him he "just doesn't understand". Perhaps he does. He tries so hard to. But it feels like I'm the only one who truly understands my own feelings on these days. I've tried putting them both down for naps. But something about today just isn't in my favour. I couldn't handle the crying from both rooms. I was torn. So, I gave in. But the crying didn't stop.

I've also been so easily triggered today. I've constantly been reminded how much is out of my control. When I walk by the state of the crumbs on the carpet for the tenth time, I feel an inner rage. Yesterday it didn't bother me.

So I've taken them for a drive, and finally after an hour they're both asleep. I don't have the radio going. I just need silence to hear myself think. This is my break today.

I repeat: Being a Stay-at-Home Mum is not the easier option.
It can be incredibly tough,
Just like every other version of motherhood.
We are all working hard.

A work of love

It feels like I spent so much time in the kitchen today, yet I hardly ate a thing.
I made snacks.
Cleaned up the snacks.
Then prepared different kinds of snacks because they didn't like the ones I made earlier.

I spent time on the kitchen floor playing with pots and pans.
Then dancing above them to their tune.
Anything so I could use both hands to prepare something I wouldn't get a chance to eat.
They had so much fun while it lasted.
I love it when they laugh together.
I get a worth-it kind of headache.

But there were fights too.
Many.
So, I'd pick up one, and distract the other.
That bought more time.

And dishes kept emerging from nowhere.
One by one they made their way back to the bench.
That was my doing.
I found them everywhere other than in the kitchen where they belong.

But that's not the only place it feels like I spent the day away.
I spent so much time in the bathroom, yet I didn't manage a shower.
Brushing teeth.
Finding their toys hidden in cupboards.
Bathing them.

And by the end of the day, they didn't want a bath.
Then when they were in, they didn't want to get out.
They tried to draw pictures with bath crayons, and I tried to keep the water from wetting the floor.
I become the fun police by this time of day.

I also spent what felt like hours in their bedrooms doing a variety of things, but mostly either helping them get to sleep or setting up quiet time.
Yet still, I didn't manage the same for myself.
Definitely not the sleep part anyway.

I'd also change their nappies there, dress them in yet another set of clean clothes and load their drawers with more.
Then I'd watch the sleeping part for what always feels like "too long".
Why does it feel like that?
Anyway, that was the closest I came to resting today.

It feels like I've spent so much time inside the same four walls today, doing the same things as I did yesterday, without much time for me.
Because I have.
And sometimes when I'm overly tired, the relentlessness of it all can make me feel like a slave in my own home.
But I'm not.
Not even close.

I'm someone else's home right now.
That's not slavery.
That's a work of love.

A late start

I put them to bed.
But that's not the end of the day.
Not even close.
Sometimes it feels like the start.
I tend to the mess first.
There's always so much mess.
It's a mess of fun, learning and love, but it's hard to see it like that at
this point.
I put the toys away.
Down on my knees, one by one, I put them back where they came from.
I crawl around the floor finding them - they're always spread so wide.
I put books back on shelves.
I fold sheets used for forts, and rearrange cushions used as jumping
mats.
I then tackle the washing pile.
The washing is endless.
I fold it into piles as I tell my husband how tired I am.
He's doing the dishes at the sink.
He's not doing it quickly enough though.
It's been a tough day.
He doesn't get it.
I tell him all of that too.
I'm always at my worst at this time.
But I don't tell him that.
Why's it so hard to admit to them?
I then put another load of washing on.
I think "didn't I just wash this?"
Or "where did all of this washing come from?"
Then I tidy up some emails, while my husband does the same.
And then I encourage him to go to bed.
I tell him "I'll be there soon".
But I'm not,
Not always.

There's still more. There's always more.
I sweep the kitchen.
Then vacuum sometimes.
I know I don't need to.
"What's the point?" I ask myself.
But I crave some order.
And when all that's done, I sit in the quiet by myself on my phone for far
too long.
But it feels too short.
And then I see the time.
And feel guilty for not spending time with him.
And for the added tired my children will get tomorrow.
But I so needed this. Boy did I need this!
I then check on the children.
I watch them for a while.
"They're so perfect", I think.
I leave washing piles outside of their rooms.
Brush my teeth.
Fall into bed beside him.
But I don't fall asleep,
Not straight away.
I overthink.
Then scroll some more.
Then toss and turn.
Then go to the loo, again.
And when I'm finally asleep, it's not for long.
It's never for long.
Because I'm called upon.
So, I'm up again,
When it's not even close to morning.
And I think to myself,
"I just should've gone to bed earlier."

Before the aftermath

Although it can be hard to see, mothering is so much more than cleaning up the aftermath.

With every toy you put away, there was fun that was had.

With every crumb that you wipe, there were hungry tummies that were fed.

With every finger smudge you clean, there was wonder that was found.

With every piece of laundry that you fold, there were little bodies that were clothed.

With every floor that you vacuum, there were feet that danced there.

So next time you feel consumed by the aftermath of housework, remember the main event.

That's where the most important work takes place.

That's where the foundations of their childhood are found, and where the depth of your mothering remains.

- You are more than the aftermath

Imagine

Imagine if you could sit and watch yourself with your children all day, and then all night.

Imagine how much you would notice that you don't when you're in the thick of doing it.

Imagine all of those things which seem so small, which objectively add up to something huge.

The time spent not stopping for a single minute.

The time spent starting to fall asleep to be awoken again.

The time you are giving to loving them before loving yourself.

You are giving so much.

You are doing so much.

Trust me, you are not imagining it.

CHAPTER FIFTEEN

WORKING-ON-TOP-OF-MOTHERING-MOTHER

When you re-enter the workforce after having been at home with your children, you have so much to offer. You are an asset to those lucky enough to work with you. Don't sell yourself short.

Reclaiming parts of her

I can still remember the day I reclaimed parts of myself.
The day I was no longer asking myself "where has she gone?"
The old me.
The one who was high-functioning.
The one who wouldn't forget what day it was.

My daughter was six months old at the time.
I'd never felt such purpose in my entire life.
My children ARE my purpose.
But for weeks I'd been feeling like part of me had left without having
time to farewell it:
My brain.

I'd been struggling to discuss much in depth like I used to, and I would
barrage my husband with simple questions I didn't know the answers to
at any given chance.
And although my brain was still very much there, and active, and
working in one of the most important ways that is nurturing a child, I
found myself craving some of the mental depth I used to have.

So on this day, I sat behind my laptop for the first time in months and I typed for an hour.
And when I read what I wrote, tears dropped onto the keyboard.
Not because of the words written, but because I realised my brain was still there.
I was still there.

So I kept writing.
And those tears that turned into words on my laptop eventually turned into a blog.
And that blog has subsequently turned into two books.

And here I am now.
The newer version of me as a mother at home with my children, with books full of poems dedicated to finding some of the lost pieces of me again; my children and I lost in the boxes of them daily.
And I've never felt more content.

So if you feel a little lost right now, or like you crave some of the old you back, please know it's perfectly normal.
It's not something to feel shame or guilt about.
You can love motherhood more than anything, but still miss some things from your life before.
And there's no pressure to find those pieces either.
Know that they'll always be there, waiting for you to be ready to find them again.

Dreams awake

After I have put my children to bed, I look in the mirror for what seems like the first time all day.
I look like the day has sucked the life right out of me.
I look like a shell of what I was this morning.
I look like I need a minute's peace, a shower, a haircut, and a good 12 hours of sleep, at the very least.

But I look like this because this is my reality.
Because I have given everything to them today.
I do every day, because they are my everything.
And I happily have my energy sucked out of me each day for them, because they give me life.
They are the most important part of my life right now.

But my life doesn't stop after their bedtime.
I carry on.
I tidy the house.
I get the washing in.
I sort life admin.
I sort all the things I couldn't sort during the day because my focus was on them.
And there can be a lot to sort.
And I can be up really late.
And the woman in the mirror at that time can look in need of a lot more.

But that's still not the end of my day.
Then I work on my own dreams.
For however long I can keep my eyes open.
And I do this for me.
Because I still have my own dreams.
Because they make me want to dream bigger.

So here's to the mothers adding to the tired when it feels like there's no more tired left to give.
Here's to the mothers who start large parts of their day after their children's day ends.
Here's to the mothers working on their own dreams while their little ones are dreaming late at night.

I see you.
You may feel lifeless right now, but your dreams matter too.
You should be so proud of yourself.
And one day they will be so proud of you.
Keep going!

The mum they need

The guilt, oh the guilt, that comes from working on top of mothering.
It's relentless.
A constant battle I didn't realise I was asking for.
One of the hardest feelings to sit with.

And all mothers are working mothers, however that looks,
Make no mistake.

And we definitely all feel guilt,
Without question.

And our levels of guilt will vary from mother to mother,
Of course.

But for me, my guilt has increased even further having transitioned from being solely a Stay-at-Home-Mother to a Stay-at-Home-Mother-while-Working-from-Home-Mother.

Whenever I need to work on top of or around my motherhood duties, I feel like I'm somehow failing them, that I am somehow not giving them enough.

Whenever I am working late into the night when the children are finally asleep, I either feel like I'm letting my house go, or my husband down. Neither ask, but I know they need my attention too.

And too often when my children are being looked after by someone else so I can work, I feel that heavy familiar hold of "they need you more". I hear the voices telling me that I'm being "selfish". I question everything. In these moments, it feels like I can't win.

And I forget.
I forget that I need this for me.
I forget that working in this way is another way of supporting my family.
I forget that I am a better mother to my children, wife to my husband, and friend to myself, when I feel a sense of fulfilment outside of motherhood.

Guilt has a way of making you forget your why, and focusing on your maybe.
It fuels your doubts, and dampens your desires.
It feels impossible to overcome some days.
Maybe it is.
I'm not sure.

But what I am sure about is this:
I care about my children so much it's crippling.
I am constantly doing what I can to be the best for them.
They are my why.

And I'm sure that's where the focus needs to be.
Because regardless of whether I work on top of mothering them, they are the factors that make me the mum they need.

A heavy load

I know that you're trying
To give the best you can
To be the mum they need
A support to your clan

I see you late at night
In the early mornings too
Sometimes in the car
And even on the loo

Utilising every second
That you can barely find
To finish what you've started
To quieten your mind

Whether that be work
Or your duties as a "mum"
The load is so heavy
Your feet can feel numb

Yet you keep running
Rushing to the next thing
Your life is in fast forward
It's always in full swing

Whether it's a choice
Or something just for you
You're supporting your family
With what you need to do

And that feeling of defeat
Because you can't do it all?
That's unfair, impossible
There are too many balls

You are just one person
With two hands and two feet
You are working miracles
Even in your sleep

Because there's no "off"
No time to catch your breath
You're at capacity, always
Your tired so in-depth

I see you Working Mama
You're an amazing mum, okay?
Even if sometimes
Your work gets in the way.

CHAPTER SIXTEEN

MOTHERING THE MOTHER

You are important. You are valuable. You are worthy of rest.
You are important. You are valuable. You are worthy of rest.
You are important. You are valuable. You are worthy of rest.
You are important. You are valuable. You are worthy of rest.
Repeat until you take a break.

More than physical

Tired in motherhood is more than physical.
Tired is physical, emotional, and psychological.
Tired is thinking, feeling and carrying the emotional weight of your children, your family, your life.
Caring so much is heavy.
Loving so hard is heavy.
Motherhood is heavy.
Some days it's more of one form than the other.
Some nights it's all forms at once.
But every form of tired is valid.

Fragile

Here's to the mums who want a break, or need a break, or ask for a break, or are offered a break, or organise a break, but for whatever reason just cannot get a break.

It's no wonder you are showing cracks right now.

That you are shattered by the end of the day.

That you feel at breaking point often.

It's hard doing anything without a break, even the things you love doing more than anything.

And it's even harder when you are hard on yourself about everything.

Be gentle.

You are fragile right now.

Handle yourself with care.

Hamster wheel

I've never had to care for myself so much, yet it feels like I don't have the time.
Every day I'm on a hamster wheel giving my all.
Round and round we go.
I'm making it all spin for them and we are making ground, so much ground, but it's hard to see some days.

I feel like my foundations are shaking.
I haven't shaved my legs in weeks.
I like getting my eyebrows done, but the space between getting them done and needing them done again seems far too short right now.
So, I rarely bother.
Any time I've been to the doctor, it's been an appointment prompted by my children's needs first, and me joining in second.
And the dentist, well that's another story.

And that's just the physical aspects of this thing called self-care.
I can't remember the last time I read a few chapters of a book without falling asleep early on, or having to re-read most of them again to catch up when I get another chance.
I can remember the last time I had a bath.
It was last week.
It was not relaxing.
It was shortened by a baby who woke an hour after bedtime.
I don't meditate, but I always think I should start.
The closest I come to deep breathing is late at night when the house is finally clean(ish), and I lie down to try to sleep.
But then it turns shallow again, as anxiety around when I will next be up creeps in.

And I can feel the shake of this all.
I know self-care is important.
But honestly, most days I can rarely do up the button on my pants or tie my hair in a bun before having to tend to something they need.
They need so much.
So much from me that by the time I have time for me, I'm often too tired for it or I have to use my last bit of energy to tend to everything that needs to be finished, like work emails that can't wait, or washing that has been needing my attention for days.

So, I wait.
My needs often wait.
And it's not ideal.
But motherhood is not always an ideal world.

And being this way doesn't always mean martyrdom either.
It can simply mean that there's a mother trying to find time for herself, in a chapter of time largely dictated by those who need her most.

One more thing

"I'll just do this one more thing."
These are the words I internalise every time I get a moment of not being needed, no matter how long or short.
Normally during nap time, moments of peaceful play, or when they are plonked in front of a cartoon.

"Just this one more dish in the dishwasher."
"Just this one more load of washing hung on the line."
"Just this one more room to vacuum."
"Just this one more surface to wipe."
"Just this one more email."
"Just this one more phone call."
"I'll just do this one more thing...
Before I have a break."
"Just this one more thing...
Before I do so much as go to the toilet."
"Just this one more thing...
Before I do something as important as eating before 2pm."

But the break doesn't come.
Not this way.
Not if I keep doing "just one more thing".
Because I'm too busy doing all of these "just one more" things, which add up to a whole lot of things, which becomes a list of a whole lot of never-ending things.
And then this "just one more thing" becomes nothing,
At least as it relates to me, and my needs.
Because trying to do everything means I've done nothing for myself.
Not within the moments of opportunity.
Not within the day which turns into night.
But it is within my control,
Always.

So, I'm trying to flip this.
I'm always trying to flip this.
I'm trying to say, I need to have "just one more hot drink", or "just one more minute for me", or "just one more minute to not be counting down the minutes and doing all the things before they need me".
I'm trying to make myself do "just one thing" for myself before doing "just one more thing" for everyone else.
Because I need me to.
And because they need me to, too.

So today I'm having one more coffee while everything that really doesn't matter is screaming at me to finish it.
Today I'm telling every "just one more thing" to wait.
Because it can,
But when I have the opportunity for my own time, I shouldn't always have to.

Just because

Just because it's a lovely day outside, doesn't mean you need to take your children out to enjoy it.

Just because it's a miserable day outside, doesn't mean you need to make the most of it and spend all day catching up on housework.

Just because the children are finally asleep, doesn't mean you need to utilise the time to finish everything you haven't had a chance to all day.

Just because someone else is looking after your children for a while, doesn't mean you need to prioritise your to-do list over things that bring you joy.

Just because it looks like everyone else is doing everything, doesn't mean you need to.

Mama, you are allowed to rest,
Just because.

Recharging

I sit there in the quiet
For the first time all day
In the middle of anywhere
Time passing my way

It can be in a car park
Or outside my home
It doesn't need to be flash
Just a safe, quiet zone

I hear them behind me
As they breathe out their sleep
The engine still running
So their dreams stay deep

I feel my shoulders relax
And the calm wash over me
As I feel my own pulse
And the wheel on my knee

There is no one grizzling
Or needing something done
It's just me and myself
Breaking from being Mum

So I open up my phone
And do nothing but scroll
Getting lost in everything else
Deep down a rabbit hole

And when I hear a stir
I'm stopped in my tracks
I look in the rear-view mirror
Feeling anything but relaxed

"Please stay asleep", I think
"I need a little longer
To catch up with myself
To get a little stronger"

And when they do relax
And settle back to sleep
I carry on doing nothing
Without hearing a peep

It's not an ideal setting
For self-care to take place
But it's all I manage some days
When time moves at pace

So here's to the mothers
Parked up, engines on
Enjoying the quiet backseats
Before it's been and gone.

Say yes to you

Mama,
When you get help with your children,
Whether that's per day, per week or just whenever it's offered,
Please know that you don't have to do every single thing you still haven't
done since too long ago.
You're allowed to have a break.
You're allowed to stop doing everything.
You're allowed to not do a single thing.
Give yourself permission.
Say yes to you.
Let others look after them so you can look after yourself.
You need looking after too.

My own

My days are largely dictated by nap times, meal times, play time, toilet time, quiet time, tummy time, family time, quality husband time, bedtimes, cleaning time, work time, not enough time, time that is not always mine to have.
So when I get time, some time, any time,
No matter what time of day or night, or what setting it takes place in,
I take my time.
I utilise every second.
I add even more time when I can.
Because this time is sacred.
It is time that is not dictated.
It is time that is my own.
It is time that reminds me I am still my own,
Even though I am a mother too.

 - Take your time

Meeting her needs

What mothers need:
To be thanked for the little things
To know that what they do matters
To be offered support without having to ask
To be encouraged to take regular breaks
To be asked how they are doing
To be told that they are doing a good job
To know that they are not alone

What mothers don't need:
To have their needs forgotten or disregarded

What everyone needs to remember:
Mothers' needs are a priority
When their needs are met, they have a better chance of meeting
their children's needs to the best of their ability.

CHAPTER SEVENTEEN

THE SISTERHOOD

Find mum friends who understand that you will probably be late to meet them for coffee (because, kids), spend the first 20 minutes talking about how tired you are (because, kids) and then have to leave early (because, kids).

The stranger who saw me

This is what supporting a mother looks like.

It looks like a complete stranger seeing my exhaustion, picking up the children's toys from underneath the chairs and bringing them back to me, without waiting to see me struggling, or me having to politely ask.

A completely new set of hands, bringing me water from the dispenser, without knowing how parched I was or how long I had been without eating or drinking a single thing.

A completely refreshing approach taken by someone I didn't expect, asking if she could help me by trying to get my fussy eight-month-old baby to sleep so I could have a much-needed break, or nap, or in her words "anything I need".

I needed her more than she will ever know that night.
And it was more than the physical help our situation screamed for.
It was about feeling seen.

Because I was more than the mother who didn't have things under control.
I was more than the mother on the floor trying to rest her eyes with two children crawling all over her at 2am at the ferry terminal, the ferry delayed, after hours in the car beforehand and hours in the car yet to come.
I was more than the mother who could only just continue to cope, not conquer.

I was a person.
A person who needed a hand.
And she saw that.

She was a stranger, but she got my baby who normally needs me to help him to sleep, to do so, on her own.
He stayed asleep on her for half an hour.
And I did nothing other than watch them in front of me in peace, eyes open but arms resting.

She was a stranger, but she was the silver lining that night.
She lightened the load.
She breathed life into me.
She kept me going.

And even though I now only have her name and a photo, I'll never forget her.
She was the stranger who saw me.

Knowing each other

I didn't know her, but she told me to go before her in the queue, a crying baby hanging off me.

I didn't know her, but she offered me her baby wipes in the public toilets, a fluster of forgetfulness overwhelming me.

I didn't know her, but she helped me pack my groceries into the car, my hands tangled up in my children beneath me.

I didn't know her, but she smiled at me as if she'd been there, an empty pram approaching her and a child in my arms trying to escape me.

I didn't know her.
And she didn't know me.
Yet we knew each other really well.
So well, that we didn't need an introduction.
We knew each other through motherhood.

Alone in love

Motherhood.
Even when you are in the best company all day, and feel touched out by the deepest form of human connection you will ever experience,
You can still feel lonely.
You can still miss adult discussions and connection outside of your mothering.
You can still count down the minutes until your partner gets home, your next play date, or your scheduled FaceTime.
You can still find yourself talking the ear off whoever turns up on your doorstep unannounced, or being comforted by a reply message at 3am.
Because mothers need connection.
We need to feel like we are not alone.
We need to know that we are not alone in our periodic loneliness.
So keep checking in with her.
Give her the opportunity to connect.
Remind her that she's never alone.

night saver

The nights can feel lonely
As you sit in the dark
With your little one on you
Resting on your heart

And even though it's special
Time you'll always treasure
Sometimes in the hard
You can't feel much pleasure

You count down the hours
Of sleep you may not get
Worrying about the day
That hasn't started yet

And as you move with them
Trying to stay awake
You wonder "is it just me
Up again tonight this late?"

You open up your phone
To see who else is there
Waiting for that dot
Beside their name to appear

You send them a message
Not caring for the time
Seeking some solidarity
Or space to have a whine

And when they do respond
No matter what they say
You know you're not alone
That you ARE doing okay

With that it feels lighter
Like your struggle is shared
It's easier not knowing
When you'll get back to bed

It's then that you realise
The ones who save your nights
Are those with you online
Tired behind screen lights.

A shared normal

She told me what she was feeling first,
And I breathed out the relief of not being alone.
Before seconding her,
And then telling her more.
Her first gave me the permission I needed,
And my second gave her the comfort she didn't know she wanted.
Suddenly, nothing felt as big, or as worrisome, or as problematic,
For either of us.
Suddenly, it all just felt normal.

    - The power of sharing

Life's answer phone message

If there were such a thing as life's answer phone message, mine would look something a little like this right now:

> *"I'm sorry I can't come right now, I'm busy caught up in them. They need me more than anyone else at the moment and my focus is showing up for them. I'll get back to you if I remember and as soon as I can. But if I forget, please don't take it personally. You are still an important person in my life. I just can't be there for everyone all the time. Please keep calling. It means so much."*

A special bond

There can be a loneliness in motherhood.
But not of love.
The days are filled with the best kind of love.

The loneliness comes from missing other adults, and mature conversations.
Your days become dictated by the needs of those who hang off of your every breath.
Plans that have been made months in advance are often put on hold, because children are sick, or too tired, or you have everything else you still need to catch up on since last week because of the same.
Staying home is often easier, even though not seeing another adult throughout the day, or outside of work, can be immensely hard.

In this season you find yourself craving connection more than any other time in your life, even though you have never felt so connected, or in love, before.
Friendships are so needed. So valued. So much of your motherhood.
But they are not the conventional type anymore.

It's friendships formed through forgotten nappies, meltdowns in the mall, and your overfriendly child.
It's friendships built on lukewarm coffee, biscuits from the packet, and messages sent at all hours of the night.
It's friendships lasting through missed coffee dates, conversations cut short, and never enough time.

All friendships are special.
But you hold these ones particularly close to your heart during this time in your life.

It's knowing that someone else just gets it.
It's knowing that someone else may be able to help you piece together parts of your sentences you may have forgotten in the fog.
It's knowing that your children have another mother in your formed sisterhood.

It's a lot of things,
But most of all it's the comfort that comes from knowing a friendship has been created from a place of such shared vulnerability during some of the hardest days of your life, a place where you have no energy to be anyone but yourself, a place where you are accepted exactly as you are and in all forms.

This is why some of the greatest friendships are formed in motherhood. And why many of these friendships last forever.

CHAPTER EIGHTEEN

FOR YOU (AND YOU KNOW WHO): JUDGEMENT AND SHAME

Reminder: You do not need to justify your parenting decisions to make others feel comfortable. That is not your role. Your role is to mother and be comfortable in the knowledge that you are doing what's best for you and your child.

Flying high

I felt helpless as we were crammed into the seat with him awkwardly over my lap.
He arched his back and kicked out every time he saw my smile covered by a mask,
Every time I tried to latch him,
Every time the air hostess offered something,
Every time someone made a noise,
For almost every moment of the time we were restrained in the air,
And it felt like the longest time.

Every moment I had a brief reprieve from the cries, I would whisper to the stranger next to me, "I'm sorry".
Because I felt that way.
I felt sorry for her and everyone else on the plane.
I don't like inconveniencing others, even when things are out of my control.

And I felt a bit sorry for myself.
Because I was having a hard time, even though I told myself "everyone's been here before".

But I mostly felt sorry for him.
My little guy who felt so distressed.
My little boy who was having such a hard time, the hardest of everyone and whose cries were not to inconvenience, but to express how hard of a time he was having.

Not being able to see the familiar smile, now covered by a mask, would have been unusual for him. And although I broke the rules and let my smile show at times, it was still hard for him.

Not being able to be walked around in familiar territory, now surrounded by unknown faces and noises all within close proximity would have been unsettling for him. And although I tried everything, it was still hard on him.

He was having a hard time. A really hard time.

And I know I shouldn't have apologised to the lady next to me.
Because babies cry.
My baby felt distressed.
And there was no inconvenience to anyone other than my own feelings.
But it's hard not to worry about being judged sometimes for the hard your child is going through.
No matter how much you tell yourself or others tell you not to.
No matter how many times you're told "we've all been there".
No matter what.

I think it's one of the hardest parts of parenting.
Letting go of feeling judged.
Letting go of expectations.
Letting go of caring about what everyone else may (or may not) think.
And I think it's okay to admit that.
Even if that's hard too.

Showing up for them

A mother is often running late.
No matter how early she started getting her children ready.
Or how prepared she was the night before.
Because there are so many things that are out of her control right now.
Things still needing to be done, and undone.
Things still needing to be redone after everything she has done in an attempt to get there on time.
And chances are she hasn't even done a single thing for herself in that rush.
That the only time she's had to take a breath has been in the car on the way to being late.
That she's then tried to sort herself in the car to not look late in the few minutes she doesn't have before arriving even later.
So when you see a mother turning up late, acknowledge her efforts.
See what came before the late.
Thank her for showing up.
Because her late is often the result of showing up for her children on time and barely showing up for herself at all.
Her late is often pushing through the easier option which would have been to just stay home.

Serving him

"He's not sleeping through yet", I tell them,
But only when they ask.
I don't have the energy to deal with this topic most of the time right now.

Some say what they think.
"Have you tried sleep training?"
"Our baby slept through at six weeks, we put her down drowsy but awake."
"He's manipulating you."
"I've only had good babies, so I can't imagine what you are going through."
Some don't say a thing, but their facial expressions say more.

And I used to try and justify myself.
Offer them some sort of explanation as to why my baby isn't (in their words) a "good baby", like (in everyone else's apparent opinion) he "should be".
"It's been too hot recently."
"He's been teething."
"He's going through a leap."
I felt compelled to, even though the real reason is much different.
Even though the real, and only reason that actually matters, is that he is just not ready yet.

This is what happens when judgement and shame are imposed on you, or the general expectation everywhere you look is that a baby should sleep through the night within the first few months.

But what a disservice.
To my baby, who will soon be a toddler, and my motherhood.
Because he is "good" even if he doesn't sleep through.
He is struggling with getting to sleep on his own.
He wants me to be with him, and help him, day and night.

And because my motherhood isn't determined by my child's milestones.
My motherhood isn't meant to look like everyone else's.
My motherhood is about doing what's best for my family.

My baby is where he needs to be, and I'm meeting him there.
I owe it to him to believe it.
I owe it to myself to trust it.
But I owe it to no one to prove it.

Your heart's work

You are entitled to protect your motherhood.
And you should.
It is your space, your home, your heart's work.
Others can be invited in, sure.
But only with your consent.
Because you hold the key.
Your motherhood should be free from judgement.
It should be your safe space to love.
It should be exactly as you need it to be.
So do what you need to protect it.

Consequences

I was up all night with him on me, feeding every hour or less.
And I'm not complaining about that.
Because I love breastfeeding.
And I'm so grateful that I can.
And I genuinely want to continue for as long as I feel like it's best for us.

But the reality of nights like this is:
I didn't get a wink of sleep.
Not that I can remember anyway.
And I'm exhausted today.
I feel this course through my bones.
And I'm a little touched out.
Actually I'm probably a lot touched out.
And I just hope he will have a gigantic nap today at some point so I can
regroup and recharge for as long as I can before we are one again for as
long as he needs that.

But this isn't complaining either.
Not in my view anyway.
This is me talking about a consequence.
A consequence of an act.
A very beautiful but often very time-consuming and draining act.
Because there is always a consequence, positive and not so positive with
any act, motherhood related or not.
But in motherhood, this is so often forgotten. And consequences are
considered as complaints.

Here's what I think.

When I talk about being exhausted because of a teething baby, I'm not complaining. I'm talking about a consequence of having a sore and needy teething baby.

When I talk about wanting bedtime to come quickly on any given day because my toddler has been struggling with her emotions since she woke, I'm not complaining. I'm talking about a consequence of having a toddler who can't regulate her own emotions yet while I'm trying to regulate mine.

When I talk about the mess and unfinished business everywhere I look, I'm not complaining. I'm talking about a consequence of being at home with two very little children who need every part of me every day.

I think we can talk about the hard without complaining.
I think we can talk about the not so positive without being ungrateful.
I think we can talk about the CONSEQUENCE as simply that.

Because every act has a consequence, but not every consequence is a complaint.

Here's to talking about the consequences.

Light and shade

If a mother talks about the hard, it doesn't mean there wasn't the easy.

If a mother talks about the imperfect, it doesn't mean there wasn't the perfect.

If a mother talks about the beautiful, it doesn't mean there wasn't the ugly.

If a mother talks about the wins, it doesn't mean there wasn't the struggle.

And her shining light on the good isn't throwing shade on anyone else, or their parenting decisions, or their experiences.

In just the same way that her sharing the shades of the darker parts doesn't mean that she can't see all of the light shining outside, or through the cracks, or everywhere she looks.

There's light and shade in motherhood.
And even if she doesn't always talk about both at once,
There's always both.

The power of listening

I don't need you to tell me that my bump is too big or too small.
I need you to hear me tell you how it's been making me feel.

I don't need you to tell me I look tired or worn out.
I need you to hear me tell you how tired I am.

I don't need you to tell me to sleep when the baby sleeps.
I need you to hear me tell you how overwhelmed I feel.

I don't need you to tell me to ignore my baby crying.
I need you to hear me whisper to you how my day's been while I cuddle them to sleep.

I don't need you to tell me to enjoy every moment.
I need you to hear me tell you about what went wrong today.

I don't need you to tell me what you think will work best for my baby.
I need you to hear me tell you what's not working for us at the moment.

I don't need you to tell me to wait for it to get harder.
I need you to hear me tell you what I'm enjoying right now.

I don't need you to ask me if my baby is a "good" baby.
I need you to hear me tell you about everything that makes my baby perfect to me.

I don't need you to tell me all of the good parts of your motherhood back when.
I need you to hear me tell you all of my hard, now.

I just don't need you to tell me, okay?
I mostly just need you to hear me.

Please listen.

Scar

When a mother shares something vulnerable about her journey with
you, or tells you how hard some aspect of her mothering has been, or
outlines what hasn't been working for her children, please don't tell her
how much success you have had with what she's struggling with, or how
great your day has been, or just how much you cannot relate to whatever
she is feeling.
That is to rub salt into a wound she hoped to heal through exposing it to
some fresh air, often before it was ready.
Instead, please listen.
And if you can't relate, or don't want to admit that you can,
Please just breathe out the air and say nothing at all.
Because words matter,
And the incorrect use of them can scar.

Depths of her motherhood

Imagine I've just shown you a photo of a woman wearing baggy, stained clothing and an upside-down smile, with tired hanging off her, no makeup on, mess surrounding her and children all over her.

Based on what you see,
Could you tell?
Could you tell that this woman used to wear heels, suits, and makeup every day?
That her work was her life?
That the weekdays consumed her?
That she enjoyed the hustle, bustle, and deadlines?
And that she particularly loved being on time?

Could you tell?
Could you tell that this woman didn't know whether she wanted to be a mother at all?
That she never gravitated towards babies?
That she never considered herself to be the maternal type?
That she worried about what sort of mother she would be if she ever became one?

Could you tell?
Could you tell that this woman loves writing, fashion, and renovating homes?
That she enjoys having things for herself?
That her children are her purpose, but she has other interests she tries to find the time for?
That she is more than spewed-on clothes and the same activewear she's worn since yesterday?

Could you tell?
Could you tell that this woman feels more alive than ever?
That the exhaustion she wears is misleading?
That she's tired, yes, but the reason she keeps going is them?
That they are her fuel, her spark, her everything?

Could you tell?
Could you tell that this woman is more than a mother?
That she's also a wife, a friend, a sister, a daughter, a cousin, a human?
That her life didn't start or end here?
But that being a mother is where she feels most at home?
And that they are where her heart will always be?

Could you tell?
Could you tell from a photo, by passing her in the street or by hearing
someone else's version of her, that she is more than a photo, a moment,
the immediate summation that you may come to?

Possibly,
But probably not.
You simply can't tell a mother's story from a glimpse, a snapshot, a tiny
snippet of what she does or does not share.
Conclusions should not be made based on what she is or is not wearing,
what she is or is not driving, how hard or not she says this season is.
Conclusions should not be made at all.

Every mother has a story,
But that story is hers and only hers to tell.
Because only she knows who she was, who she is, and who she is
becoming.
Only she knows the depths of her motherhood

CHAPTER NINETEEN

For you both: Partners in parenting

Parenting changes you, as individuals and as a couple. It will unravel parts of you that you haven't seen yet, and close off some of the parts that brought you together in the first place. But with change comes growth. And that growth can lead you to form some of the strongest foundations you will ever build together.

Our stay

I loved you before them.
But with them between us now, I love you even more.

Because we have been through so much together since them, because of them, with them.
Because while parenthood has tested our love, it has shown us a new love worth working for.
Because you show up for me, and them, and you never leave when pushed.

You stay.
You have always stayed.
You are the stay of us, our family.

You have seen me at my worst, my weakest, my most challenging of moments and most tired in years.
Through pregnancies,
Through births,
Through postpartum.
Yet you hold my hand even tighter.

And you have worn my hard days.
Just as you wear them.
On your chest,
On your shoulders,
On your heart.
You carry them too, and relish in the weight of all that they are.

You have been there with me, in moments of them needing me, because
I needed someone too.
Holding me, while I hold them.
Feeding me, while I feed them.
Consoling me, while I console them.
You have been my someone when I've felt like everyone.

And you make their smiles shine even brighter. The only way you know
how. Your own way.
With your jokes,
And your play,
And all the things I don't have the energy for by 5pm.
You are why they don't want to go to bed,
And why the weekends can't come fast enough.

You are their light.
Just as you have always been mine.
But as a Dad you shine even brighter.

Bound by love

Us,
We are still bound by love.
But it's a changed love.

It's the mornings started too early with them all over us.
It's the echoes of stories being read to them between walls separating us.
It's the offerings of sleep-ins without the other.
It's the way we call each other first when we see them have a first.
It's the smiles we save for them, and the worry for them that we share between us.
It's the holding of them to allow the other to eat a hot meal.
It's then swapping so we both get fed.
It's the handholds in the car while they sleep in the back, being the first quiet moment had together in weeks.
It's the vacuuming late at night.
It's asking, "how was your day?"
It's saying, "I'm grateful for you".
It's remembering, "we are a team".
It's listening to complaints and offering a shoulder.
It's sitting next to each other and understanding that silence is needed.
It's falling asleep together while scrolling for something to watch.
It's the tears wiped, and backs rubbed in the short time we share our bed alone.
It's the disagreements fuelled by caring too much.
It's then carrying on parenting when we haven't quite got over it.
It's forgiveness before we close our eyes each night.
It's wearing the ageing tired together, and seeing only the beauty.
It's the strength found through sharing the hard.
It's hardly seeing each other, but feeling closer than ever.
It's the less of the "us" and more of the "them".

Us.
We are still bound by love.
But it's a changed love.
A love that can be hard to recognise.
A love that isn't always easy.
A love of growth.
But it's a very special love,
Because it's love of us, for them.

A few words

It was 8pm.
Both children were still wide awake.
I was only just keeping my eyes open.
The day had been so long.
With one sick, and the other one having to stay inside all day because it was raining.

My youngest had been on my person since the night prior.
My eldest was frequently on my case to do something because she was "bored".
I'd tried to get them to bed early on my own.
That did not work.
Some nights it does.
But not tonight.

I decided while they were still awake, I'd start cleaning up so I would have more time to myself once they finally did go down.
The toys were tipped out of the box almost immediately after I'd put them away.
Milk was spilt on the floor.
I couldn't find the bottle.
I'd snapped at the puppy.
She'd dragged clumps of dirt through the house.
And it wasn't the first time.

I was getting short with them for having fun so late, and then feeling guilty for the same.
I could feel my temper bubbling at the surface, waiting for something completely minute to set me over.
I held it in.
I was holding onto so much, on very little.

Like we all do.
I just needed them to go to bed.

And then my husband walked through the door.
The children raced to him, leaving me a grumpy wound-up lump on the floor.
They were so excited to see him.
I was excited he was home too, but for mostly different reasons.
And that right there was the minute detail.
It set me off.
I escaped to my room and sobbed out the bits I needed to.

And this is a summary of what I later told my husband:
They push me more than you, and it's so hard.
They get bored of me because they see me all day.
You come home and see them happy, and it probably makes it hard to believe I did have a hard day.
It was a hard day.
It can be difficult to enjoy them as fully as I'd like on days like this.
And then I feel so guilty for not.
I love them so much.

He rubbed my thigh, and said a number of things,
But what I mostly remember him saying was "I know", and "it must be so hard",
Because that was all I needed to hear.

All we need

"You just don't get it", I tell him
I'm so tired I can't think straight
I've been feeding our baby all night
I need sleep, not to be awake

"You just don't get it", I tell him
I've seen no one else all day
It can feel really lonely sometimes
Please hear what I've got to say

"You just don't get it", I tell him
I don't like being touched right now
I've been crawled over since breakfast
I need myself for an hour

"You just don't get it", I tell him
I've seen mess since this morning
I can't look at it any longer
Real anxiety is forming

"You just don't get it", I tell him
I need them to go to bed soon
I know you've hardly seen them
But I've been strung out since noon

"You just don't get it", I tell him
I don't feel like I'm seen
All the things I've done today
And everyone I've been

"You just don't get it", I tell him
It's hard being home all day
I love them so much it hurts
But I need some time away

"You just don't get it", I tell him
As I sob into his chest
"It's relentless loving this way
Selflessly, and without rest"

"You just don't get it", I tell him
"I don't", he whispers back
"I'm sorry, I'm trying", he says
Into him I start to relax

"Perhaps you're not meant to get it"
I tell him as I start to breathe
"But we get each other, don't we?"
"And maybe that's all we need."

not just still

I see you.
Oh, how I see you.
Changing nappies, making bottles, giving piggy back rides.
Finding sippy cups, reading stories, falling asleep next to them.
Playing hide and seek, brushing their hair, being their clown.

And in darkness I see you too.
In fact, I see you most then.
I have such deep need for you during those hours.
To help me, to hold my hand, to bring me into the sunlight for them,
even when I'm not ready.

I see you tending to them, being there for me, adding to your tired
tomorrow.
It means so much.

Encouraging me to go to bed earlier, checking on me at night, reaching
out for me when I return to bed.
Being who I need when I need it most.

Waking with thoughts about work, sometimes leaving before we wake,
and returning after they are in bed.
I know you are doing this all for us.

But I also know you must feel invisible some days.
I forget to tell you what I see.
I'm just so busy catching my own tail, being caught up in them, doing
what I can to mother them well.

And as we move through many of our days doing nothing other than getting through to the next, I miss you.

Oh, how I miss you.

Even though you are right there.

Even though we have never been more of a team.

Even though there's nowhere else I'd rather be than in this, with you, for them.

I wonder if you feel it too? That constant longing to reconnect, in face of one of the strongest reasons for connection we will ever know: Them.

And as we start yet another day together but at arm's length,

Know that I'm still here.

I'll always be here, even when you don't see me,

Just as you have been for me.

Know that I see you.

I miss you.

And I love you.

Oh, how I love you.

And not just still.

But even more than before.

Changing together

The truth is that parenting will change your relationship.
You will see some of the best of each other,
But also some of the worst.
You will spend a lot of time trying to find each other again,
But also getting lost in who you are becoming.
You will say "I love you" less,
But "I'm sorry" more.
And you will have to work on things.
You will constantly need to evolve, shift, and grow into who you need
to be for each other.
Because you will need each other more than ever.
The trick is finding the person who is willing to change with you.

CHAPTER TWENTY

For them: Extra love notes

My children love me exactly as I am. They pour their love into me regardless of what I look like, how much money we have, what I wear, or my likes and dislikes. They love me for me. And I will never take that for granted. I will honour it by continuing to love them for them, in all forms, exactly as they are, every day for the rest of my life.

One beautiful blend

I know you won't remember
The way we dance at night
Your body on my chest
Hands held under moonlight

Your fingertips scan my face
From my eyes to my lips
Your feet move with me
As I rock you from my hips

I know you won't remember
All the times we lie awake
Me whispering you stories
Repeatedly till day break

You try to move in closer
And you shuffle back and forth
Looking for a better spot
To enjoy our shared warmth

I know you won't remember
Me carrying you around
From early morning through till dusk
You hardly touch the ground

I scoop you up, carry on
With my one free hand
And talk you through my movements
To help you understand

I know you won't remember
The way I calm your fears
How holding you to my heart
Can wipe away your tears

Or how distressed you get
When I leave you for a while
In hands very different to mine
You seeing a new smile

I know you won't remember
How much joy you bring
Or how you've helped me grow
Into who I'm becoming

The challenges we both face
And the nights that never end
We're there for each other, always
We are one beautiful blend

I know you won't remember
Much of these early days
Often I fret I won't either
Through my sleep-deprived haze

But I promise I'll remember
These special years of us
Through photos, videos, memories
For us, one day, to discuss.

Let me tell you

Children of mine, let me tell you.
Because I need you to know.

I need you to know that every time I hold you, the world stops.
There is a quietness in our space, our togetherness, our peace.
But not in my heart.
That screams with warmth, love, and every single feeling I want to hold
onto forever.
So let me hold you longer.

I need you to know that every time I see your smile, everything wrong
feels right.
The worry disappears for a moment and my joy is set alight in flames.
It burns for as long as we spark together.
It breathes oxygen into our happiness and lightens all the heavy.
So let us keep smiling together.

I need you to know that every time I dry your tears, I soak in your need.
Your need for every piece of me. My skin, my touch, my breath.
And I exhale my love into every part of you.
It's hard being your everything sometimes but I keep going.
The hard is easier knowing I am your rainbow after the storm.
And nothing is easier than loving you.
So let me continue drying your tears.

I need you to know that every time I see your firsts, I want to hold on.
Because I'm proud. Because with every first there is a last. Because you
are ready for your firsts and I'll never be ready for your lasts.
But you will always come first.
And as you step closer into yourself and further away from me, I'll be
here.
I'll be the first to celebrate with you and the last to forget.
So let me keep seeing you grow.

I need you to know that every time you call for me, I find myself.
With your voice, your arms, your eyes of longing.
You are my calling, my purpose, my reason right now. And I am yours.
We are constantly searching for each other, lost as one but found within
ourselves.
And it's perfect. You are perfect. Nothing could be more perfect.
So let me keep searching for you.

Children of mine, let me tell you.
Because I need you to know.

Everything you are is everything I need, and more.
I just hope I can be everything for you while you need it.

Sealed with a kiss

Every night I kiss you
On your sweet little head
After the day's over
You asleep in your bed

I watch you for a moment
Sometimes longer too
My heart melts completely
I'm so lucky to have you

I think about our day
Moments stolen by my tired
Focusing on the less-than
Not everything I tried

And the guilt becomes heavy
My mind a battlefield
I replay everything over
My self-doubt revealed

But what about the rest?
The fun that we had?
The toys, the games, and love?
It can't have been that bad?

I ask myself these questions
As I sit and watch you sleep
It's silly really, I know
But my love for you is deep

This is just what happens
When you care so much
You want to offer your finest
And improve your low, as such

So I vow to do better
Despite giving my best
Before kissing you once more and
Tucking you into your nest

And while you do not see it
While you'll never know
It's important to me that I do it
Before I turn and go

Because this is my way
Of ending the day with good
Of letting the bits go
That remain misunderstood

This is how I honour
All that perfect that I missed
Before closing it with my love
And sealing it with a kiss.

My forever

I may not always be right here,
In the way I am now.
Skin to skin, breath to breath, heart to heart.
In the days, nights and everything in between.
But I'll always be here.
Just a phone call away.
Never too far away.
My heart will always be yours.

And I may not always look like this,
The way I do now.
My eyes so tired and my hair such a mess, my polish so little and my
bags so large, my body so new and my wardrobe so old.
But I will always look back at this time with such pride.
For all I did.
For all I became.
All of it was worth it for you.

And I may not always see your firsts,
In the way I can now.
First smiles and tastes, first words and steps, first firsts and lasts.
But you'll always come first.
A love that never loses.
A memory that never fades.
You are a winner in every sense.

And I may not always be the one you come to,
In the way you do now.
With your tears and laughter, your pride and confusion, your happiness
and worry.

But I'll be where you need me to be.
Second, or last.
Tomorrow or one day.
I'll always wait for you to need me again.

And I may not always be the last one you see at night,
In the way I am now.
Pages skipped and lines misread, stories exchanged and lullabies
whispered, stopping and starting every chapter.
But you will always be my favourite story.
Sentences printed on my heart.
Chapters repeated with your own.
The entire plot on the bookcase of my soul.

And I may not always carry you in my arms,
In the way I do now.
From side to side, from place to place, from day till night.
But I will always carry you.
In my heart which calls for you.
In my mind which thinks of you.
In my memories filled with every part of you.

And I may not have the privilege of being your everything,
In the way I am now.
Your comfort and dreams, your earth and sun, your moon and stars.
But I'll always have the privilege of being your mum.
The name I prefer more than my own.
The role I'll always be most proud of.
A title I'll honour forever.

My darlings,
We may not always have the way we are now.
But that's okay,
Because you will always be my forever.

An always love

I don't always love my body, but I love that it's given me you.
I don't always love getting up during the night, but I love being your answer right now.
I don't always love what the tired can turn me into, but I love who I have become because of you.
I don't always love the finger smudges on the windows, but I love the permanent mark you've left on my heart.
I don't always love how lost I feel, but I love who you are helping me find.
I don't always love coming last, but I love being first in your eyes.
I don't always love worrying about you but I love that I care so deeply.
I don't always love turning up late, but I love that it's because I'm early for you.
I don't always love the mess, but I love that it is your happiness.
I don't always love being touched out, but I love nothing more than being your home.
I don't always love missing out on things, but I love being there for you.
I don't always love stopping what I'm doing, but I love that my time is yours.
I don't always love every single moment in motherhood, but I will always, always, love you.

Just how much I love you

My hope has been for you to know how much I love you.
Not just one day, but forever.

In these early years, my love is shown in the unseen, and often the
unsaid.
It's in the games we play before sunrise and the rocking chair we share
late at night.
It's in the slowing down for you, and the rushing to make that possible
at all.
It's in my dinners that remain untouched, and my touch that remains on
demand.
It's in my nights remaining at home instead of out, and the weekends
which start to look identical.
It's in the holding of my breath, biting my tongue and pushing through
my triggers.
It's in my overthinking, my worry, my tears which turn on and off like a
tap.
It's in my showing up for you, over and over, again and again, no matter
what I may need, no matter what.
It's the little things.
The mundane things.
The things you don't even know are anything just yet.

But I know.
These things are everything.
Just as you are to me.
So I show you,
And tell you anyway,
That I love you more than you know right now.

And one day, when the years pass and they will forever feel too late, I will continue to show you and tell you.
But it will be different.
Because you will be older, and wiser, and understanding of what it is to love, and be loved.

Even so, it will remain constant.
It will be in the initiating phone calls, and accepting FaceTimes if I'm lucky.
It will be in the keeping a spare room for you, or making room whenever you need it.
It will be loving you through your hard times, your good times, and everything in between.
It will be holding your own children, those you love, and you even when you don't know you need it.
It will be in the constant reassurance that I'm not with you, but I'm still here.
It's in the thoughts.
The memories.
The quality not quantity.

It will be showing you,
And telling you,
That I love you more than you can ever know.

Because by then I will know,
That no matter how much older, wiser, and understanding of love you get,
And no matter how hard I try to show, say, and prove my love to you,
You will never truly be able to know just how much I do,
Because that's how much I love you.

CHAPTER TWENTY-ONE

FOR EVERY MOTHER: MOTHER ON

Motherhood will test you at times, but it's not an exam. There are not grades. You can never be fully prepared. The right answer one day could be the wrong answer the next. So cut yourself some slack. Let yourself learn as you go. Mother yourself free.

Taste of love

The same things taste better when someone else makes them for you.
Coffee, toast, the everyday ordinary made with the same ingredients, the
same methods, the same amount of time, but with a different pair
of hands.
And when you become a mother, you start to understand this at a deeper
level.
It tastes like thoughtfulness.
It tastes like one less thing you need to think about, do, and re-do.
It takes like your needs matter too.
But above all, it tastes exactly like what everybody else enjoys you
serving up for them every day.
Remember that Mama,
You make the ordinary taste better.

Motherhood reminders

Motherhood reminders from me to you:

You are allowed to hide in the toilet when your other half gets home, and spend way too long on your phone.

You are allowed to sit in your car and listen to the end of your podcast before you go back inside to enjoy the silence for that little bit longer.

You are allowed to buy things for yourself because you want them, not because you need them.

You are allowed to hide your favourite treats from your family to be guaranteed the taste of something you deserve.

You are allowed to drive your children around in the car for absolutely no reason other than needing a break from being needed for a while.

You are allowed to stay up too late watching Netflix knowing that you will be even more tired the next day, and then complain about being tired the next day.

You are allowed to let your children watch as much screen time as you need them to, so that you can do what you need to do.

You are allowed to skip pages of books, bath time routines and vegetables on the side of the plate some nights.

You are allowed to say "yes" to the easier options all day.

You are allowed to say "no" at any time during the day.

You are allowed to do what you want, where you want, however you want.

Because the when-you-want hardly comes these days.

Because this is your motherhood.

Because you (and only you) get to make the rules.

Courage

It takes courage to be a mother.
To hope for a chance with them, to go in completely blind, to trust in the process.
To swallow the pain, to keep trying after loss, to carry them through the storms of anxiety if you get a chance at all.

It takes courage to be a mother.
To stretch your home for someone else, to see a new reflection, to honour a new skin.
To be the gateway for life, to be torn or cut open, to endure the beautiful intensity that is birth.

It takes courage to be a mother.
To be left raw and cracked open, to bleed out the tears, to carry on for them while healing the remains postpartum.
To carry life-long injuries, to work through associated trauma, to accept postpartum is forever.

It takes courage to be a mother.
To keep facing the tired, to keep braving the hard days, to keep loving yourself through the unlovable moments.
To mute the outside noise, to be your own advocate, to listen to your intuition.

It takes courage to be a mother.
To wear your heart on your sleeve, to hear it beat outside of your chest,
to hold it in their hands.
To put your body on the line, to put your sleep on hold, to put yourself
after others.

It takes courage to be a mother.
To give everything to them today, to give even more tomorrow, to give
them the confidence to leave you one day.
To accept the magnitude of your role, to accept that you'll make
mistakes, to accept that you can't ever be as perfect as they are to you.

It takes courage to be a mother.
To step into it, to grow into it, to stay in it.
To try every single day to better the life for someone else who you love
more than life itself.

It takes courage to be a mother.
It really does.
And I encourage you to see that.

The both in motherhood

I love them,
But I'm tired.
I'm always so tired.

I'm tired from little sleep, so many emotions, the constantness of it all.
When will it end?
But please don't,
Because everything else that comes with it might end too.
Because this is such a wholesome chapter.
I'm so empty but full.

And I love them so much.
Did I mention that?
More than all the sleep I could have.
I love this chapter more than any other I've written already.
But I'm so exhausted.
Nothing has ever been so tiring.
I'd love a nap.
Or a sleep through.
Just so I can dream of them more and have more energy when I wake to them.
Because I love them.
But I'm sure I've mentioned that.

I'm so grateful for them,
But I need a break.
A holiday would be great.
Or just a day off.
And a night.
Because it's not either/or right now.
It's all hours.

But then I'd miss them.
I know I would.
I do when they're in the next room sleeping.
What is sleep again?
What was I saying again?
Sorry, mum brain.
Motherhood is strange.

But yes, it feels so strange without them.
I feel empty, and limbless.
Because we are one right now.
And I'm so grateful to experience the privilege of being their everything.
Have I said that?
I feel so honoured to have the need for a break from loving them so
much as being my biggest problem.
But they are not the problem.
Life and all its other demands are.

I love being a mum,
But it's hard sometimes.
I feel lost,
Like I'm missing parts of myself.
And time,
There's never enough time.
For anything or anyone.

But I love being a mum.
I've said that right?
Because it's the best job in the world.
It's not even work.
But it is.
Hard work.
The hardest thing I've ever done.

Yet I choose it.
Without question.
And I'd choose it over and over again.
Hard, missing pieces, never enough time included.
Because they are worth it.
The easier will come one day, and that will be harder.

I love them, I'm so grateful for them, I love being a mum.
Did I mention that already?
Because I do.
With every single fibre.
And because I can be both, of all.
In love and tired, grateful and touched out, content and lost.
We can be both, always.
Motherhood is big enough for both.

Growing away

They say it gets easier
That sleep will come
That they'll move to solids
And be walking by one

They say it gets easier
That experience will help
That you'll find your feet
Forget how hard it felt

They say it gets easier
They'll learn to talk
They'll tie their own shoes
Use a knife and fork

They say it gets easier
That the fun will start
You'll have more time
More light, less dark

They say it gets easier
Your arms will flow free
School bags on backs
Your bed now empty

They say it gets easier
You'll feel yourself again
You'll leave the house more
And remember your brain

They say it gets easier
And perhaps they're right
Practically speaking anyway
But it's not black and white

Because it doesn't feel easier
Not emotionally anyway
To have to let go
When you'd love them to stay

Because it doesn't feel easier
When they need you less
When you wait for their call
When your mind's a mess

Because it doesn't feel easier
The worry doesn't stop
They are your whole world
Your heart forever in knots

Because it doesn't feel easier
To love so much
To lean into trust
To lose your touch

Because it doesn't feel easier
No matter their stage
To see your forever babies
Grow away with age.

Holding on

It's holding on.
To time that's already passed,
To tiny arms around your neck,
And to little legs around your hips.

It's holding on.
To worry and hope in one breath,
To the little things that they've outgrown,
And to the moments of being their world.

It's holding on.
To what was, what is, and what could be,
To the edges of the hard days,
And to the easiest love you will ever know.

It's holding on.
To your partner and your friends,
To photos and tattered toys,
And to memories you fear you may forget.

It's holding on.
To so much guilt,
To a heavy load which shakes you to your core,
And to expectations of what you "should" be.

It's holding on.
To your sanity,
To pieces of your former self,
And to a new version of you, both of which they have parts of.

It's holding on.
To new skin and old jeans,
To unrealistic ideals and pressures,
And to your former reflection that won't let you let go easily.

It's holding on.
To what serves you as a family,
To what you know you need to work on for them,
And to the fragments of your mothering that don't deserve a grip.

It's holding on.
To firsts and lasts,
To moments of magic in the mundane,
And to an ache of loving so deeply.

It's holding on.
To them,
To your partner,
And to yourself, in that order.

It's holding on.
To this intensely beautiful connection,
To this fleeting chapter,
And to this new life which will leave you wanting to hold on forever.

It's holding on.
So desperately that you feel weak all over,
So tight that your knuckles turn white,
So vulnerably that your heart feels exposed.

It's holding on.
And then one day letting go.

Proud

I'm proud of her.

I'm proud of how she has stepped into her role, one she has no training for and which is far different to what she was expecting.

I'm proud of her for growing, nourishing and raising the little humans the way she is. The way that feels right. Her way.

I'm proud of how she manages each day on little sleep, too much coffee and the perfect amount of love.

I'm proud of her for showing up every day no matter what and for staying there for as long as she is needed.

I'm proud of her for honouring her new skin, her new life and her new purpose even when she feels so old.

I'm proud of her for doing all the unseen things and for seeing them before her always.

I'm proud of her for trying her best every day, even when her best looks different or feels the worst.

I'm proud of her for allowing herself to be lost in them, in this season, in everything they want and need when she's still trying to find the "her" in herself.

I'm proud of her for loving them with every inch of every part of her even when she feels that she has no more her to give.

I'm proud of her.

When I allow myself to see it this way anyway.
When I see past the clutter of everything that really doesn't matter.
When I see her with them in this way, in her current form.

I am proud of her.
I am allowed to be.
You are too.

And we should tell her more.
My her, your her, every her.
Because there's a lot to be proud of.

All that she is

I respect mothers so much more now that I am one.
I know how much work goes in.
I'm living it, breathing it, right there in the thick of it with those who have gone before me, and those walking right beside me.
I understand, at a deep level, what it is to be called "Mama", "Mummy", "Mum".

And when I see mothers going about their everyday, I'm reminded.

When I see her at the supermarket with babes on hips, and shopping bags in any spare arm, I understand what's involved. How strong her arms have become from having to carry them with every single thing she does, and how weak her patience may become in only a few more minutes. I respect how much she has going on, which may not look like much at all, because she's so good at making it look easy. But I know it's not easy.

When I see her pushing a pram at a family function away from the food, family and fun, I sense her loneliness. Her waves of resentment. Her longing for someone to offer her a hand so she can be involved in the celebrations for a bit. And I do offer a hand, always, if I have a spare. Because I respect her sacrifice. And because I know. I know she may not want my hand. Or anyone else's. But I also know she wants to be seen in her work. And to her that gesture means everything.

When I see her sitting in the plane with her baby awake on her chest, or a toddler on her lap, or both. When I see everyone around her sleeping peacefully. I feel her tired. I feel her desperation for rest. I feel how concerned she is by having her child wake the rest of the plane. I have an urge to hold her. To give her the rest. To remind her that I'm right there with her, covered in baby, a few rows back. Because I respect her. I respect how much she is giving. I respect her needs. I respect her worry for everyone else, even when they are strangers.

When I see a mother working on her dreams outside of motherhood, or lost in her dream of motherhood. When I see her squished between car seats, or changing a nappy in the car boot. When I see her in any form, mothering in her own way.

When I see her, I see myself.
And I just have so much respect for all that she is.

Only one

It won't always be like this.
I remind myself of this often.
To help me see through the hard days, but to also pull me into the now.

Because it's true.
They won't always be this small. And I won't always be this tired.
They won't always need me in this way. And I won't always feel this lost.
They won't always come to me first. And I won't also feel like I come last.

This is a season.
We will move through it together.
And it will pass before we know it.

It won't always be like this.
And my heart aches as I think about what it may look like.
The first school drop off.
The last kiss goodnight.
The nights up late waiting for a call that doesn't come.

Because life will be different one day.
And it won't always be this tiring, messy, or beautifully wholesome.
It will be watching from afar from a clean house, longing for them to come home for a weekend.
It will be loving them through phone lines, messenger, and the kilometres between us.
It will be losing myself in something new, to busy my mind from what I'm missing.

It won't always be like this.
Not the hard.
Or the beautiful.
It will be a different hard and beautiful.

We won't always be like this either.
We will age.
And our relationship will evolve.
We will be a different type of "us".

But this is my one chance at now.
I only get to love them, be there for them, and be needed in this exact way, once.
I only get to know this stage of motherhood like the back of my hand, once.
I only get this time as we are now, once.

This is it.
I only get one Motherhood.
And they only get one childhood.

This time is ours.
So I'm breathing it in, in all of its shades,
Because it just won't always be like this.

What it always will be

What I have learnt as my motherhood journey has continued:

Hold your babies. They don't spoil. Or keep. They won't always be yours to hold on to. One day before long they will be reaching for the light switches and telling you they can do things on their own. It happens before you know it, and there's no warning or going back.

Listen to your intuition before everything else, particularly what everyone tells you that you "should" be doing with your babies. You have been there since the beginning. Your heart grew them into who you birthed. And it will continue to lead you through your motherhood, and their childhood, if you let it.

Don't compare your children's milestones to others of similar ages. They are different and always will be. Trust they will get to where they need to when they are ready. They have their own timing, just like you.

Take the photos. All of the photos. Of them. Of yourself. Of the moments you may not consider worthy of documenting. One day you will long to be taken back to that time, but your memory will be foggy. You will need prompts to remind you of what you once lived. Photos will be your pathway to memories that may otherwise get lost.

Go easy on yourself. You are doing the best you can with what you know, and the energy you have, at any given moment. Your time in each stage is limited so try not to focus on the things that do not matter, like the amount of screen time they have, the convenient meals you serve, and the "it will do today" approach. They will turn out just fine. This becomes more apparent the older your children get and the more you have.

You don't give yourself enough credit. Society doesn't either. And while you can't change society, you can change how you value yourself. Don't let everything you do feel insignificant. It is making, moulding, and changing lives.

This is still hard,
Even though you know more.
Perhaps it always will be.

But it's also still beautiful.
So beautiful.
And even though it starts to look different, it always will be.

The greatest guarantee

You are never guaranteed much in early motherhood.
Not sleep,
A hot coffee,
A finished meal,
A break,
An easier day,
Or consistency of any sort most of the time.
But what you are guaranteed is love.
So much love.
Every single day.
No matter what.
And what a beautiful thing to be able to rely on.

- Mother on

You can find me on:

 @Wordsof_Emmaheaphy

 @Wordsofemmaheaphy

Printed in Great Britain
by Amazon

86130725R00150